THIS IS ME!

AMAZING WORDS

Edited By Jenni Harrison

First published in Great Britain in 2022 by:

Young Writers
Est. 1991

Young Writers
Remus House
Coltsfoot Drive
Peterborough
PE2 9BF
Telephone: 01733 890066
Website: www.youngwriters.co.uk

Printed and bound in the UK by BookPrintingUK
Website: www.bookprintinguk.com
YB0491P

FOREWORD

For Young Writers' latest competition This Is Me,
we asked primary school pupils to look inside
themselves, to think about what makes them unique,
and then write a poem about it! They rose to the
challenge magnificently and the result is this fantastic
collection of poems in a variety of poetic styles.

Here at Young Writers our aim is to encourage creativity
in children and to inspire a love of the written word, so
it's great to get such an amazing response, with some
absolutely fantastic poems. It's important for children to
focus on and celebrate themselves and this competition
allowed them to write freely and honestly, celebrating
what makes them great, expressing their hopes and
fears, or simply writing about their favourite things.
This Is Me gave them the power of words. The result
is a collection of inspirational and moving poems that
also showcase their creativity and writing ability.

I'd like to congratulate all the young poets
in this anthology, I hope this inspires them
to continue with their creative writing.

CONTENTS

Even Swindon Primary School, Raybrook Park

Kacey Bainbridge (9)	67
Jenson Bird (9)	68
Erin Giles (10)	70
Dawson Handy (10)	71
Jessica Robertson (10)	72
Finley Griffin (9)	73
Lilly Smith (9)	74
Jack Griffin (9)	75
Iziyah Windslow-Davis (7)	76
Aarohi Singh (8)	77
Jools McMahon (9)	78
Evie Wischhusen (9)	79
Evie Amelia Adkin (10)	80
Jaida Aldridge (10)	81
Olivia Blewett	82
Caleigh Marques (10)	83
Thea Elisha (10)	84
Valentina Tarosso (9)	85
Ariel Kernse (10)	86
Charlie Edwards (9)	87
Maxi S (9)	88
Ziya Rose (9)	89
Jennie Campbell (9)	90
Bethany Scott (9)	91
Jamie-Lee Tewkesbury (9)	92
Amelia Francis (10)	93
Layla Matthews (10)	94
Peri Ekiz (10)	95
Krisha Sunar (9)	96
Mason Ferguson (9)	97
Ethan Marques (7)	98
Layla Cousens (9)	99
Ollie Loveridge (9)	100
Jessica Jacobson (7)	101

Ferndale Primary School, Great Barr

Kajetan Krajewski (10)	102
Daisy Price (11)	105
D'rcy Johnson-Bryan (10)	106
Peter Vassilev (10)	109
Karanvir Singh (10)	110
Abeera Khan (10)	113
Evie Smith (10)	114
Shivam Thakur (11)	117
Roman Banga (10)	118
Olivia Arblaster (10)	121
Daawud Rassool (10)	122
Umayrah Rahman (10)	125
Louie Roberts (10)	126
Logan Heard (11)	128
Leela Harrison (10)	130
Wathma Weerasingha (10)	132
Samuel Bennett (10)	134
Zahra Rahman (10)	136
Alyaan Raja (10)	138
Maiya Chattu (10)	140
Isabel Hunter (10)	142
Jia Chaudhry (10)	145
Anna Higgins (11)	146
Jasleen Neer (10)	148
Noah Sargent (10)	150
Keanna Daniels (10)	152
Nehan Tanvir (10)	154
Tayhon Elson (10)	156
Esha Allport (10)	158
Peter Wright (10)	160
Arjan Klaar (10)	162
Juvrajan Barnes (11)	164
Ibrahim Rassool (10)	166
Maliha Zia (11)	168
Megan Pickford (11)	170
Ella Ashby (11)	172
Ethan Dodge-Pace (10)	174
Eniola Adeyemi (10)	176
Arun Dhadley	178
Calum Robinson-Ash (10)	180
Tia Williams (10)	182
Giulia Zainea (10)	184
Mikolaj Wardawa (10)	186
Lucas Smith (10)	188
Tayvia Hylton (10)	189
Mustafa Rehman (10)	190

Mazy Smith (11)	191
Isabelle Harrington	192
James Mills (10)	193
Miruna Luca	194
Jarred Jonas (10)	195
Umar Faruki (10)	196
Ashton Carr (10)	197
Poppy Rollins (10)	198
Sahar Khan (11)	199
Tiana Lugha (10)	200
Luke-Curdie Powell (10)	201
Niko Paszowski (10)	202
Adam Gardner (10)	203
Elena Smith (10)	204
Ollie Bolton (10)	205
Scarlett Aitchison (10)	206

Laira Green Primary School, Laira

Lauren Mitchell (7)	207
Layla-May Redgrave (7)	208
Elijah Romeo (8)	209
Isaiah Romeo (8)	210
Amie Grimwood (9)	211
Maddison Mouele (7)	212
Kayden Jones (8)	213
Kacey Middleton (8)	214
Noah Black (8)	215
Katie Lutley (8)	216
Freddie Baker-Truelove (7)	217
Indigo Baker (8)	218
Violet Nicholls (8)	219
Eloise Peart (8)	220
Shianna Dawson (9)	221
Leo Parker (9)	222
Ishan Dahal (7)	223
Emelia Turner (8)	224
Evie Wilde (8)	225
Honey Bolter (8)	226
Freddie Jones (7)	227
Riley	228
Emily Bogusiewicz (8)	229
Amelie Collins (7)	230
Leo Cordy (7)	231

Rogue (7)	232

McKinney Primary School, Dundrod

Alex Harkness (7)	233
Jesse Wright (7)	234
Macey Wilson (7)	235
Willow Irvine (7)	236
Eliza Bell (7)	237
Miriam Bell (7)	238
Chloe Kyle (8)	239
William Stewart (8)	240
Meadow O'Grady-Waite (7)	241
Eli King (8)	242
Reuben McKinstry (7)	243
Jonathan Simpson (8)	244
Alfie Moses (8)	245
Jack Carson (7)	246
Isaac Barber (7)	247
Layla Carlisle (8)	248
Jenson Minford (7)	249

Zakariya Primary School, Forest Gate

Arobi Asaduzzaman	250
Inamurrahman Mohammed	252
Aaishah Rahamathaullah (10)	253
Muhammad Hassan (9)	254
Azaan Al Islam Matubber	255
Mohammed Ismail (9)	256
Humaira Begum Ahmed (10)	257
Samir Mohammed (10)	258
Fatima Zahra (9)	259
Manal Said (10)	260

THE POEMS

When I'm Happy

I live at home with mom and dad, but I've got the smallest room, which makes me sad.

When I'm happy I explode in a smile, then again when I'm angry I've got teeth like a crocodile.

In the morning I spring out of bed like a cheetah, so good at computer games people think I'm an online cheater.

Oh yeah, I ride a bike like Evil Knievel over bumps, I fly high like an eagle.

Pizza and chocolate, my favourite food. Ask me for a helping, I might be rude.

Movie and snacks, my favourite pastime.

Before I sleep I read a book, then leave on the nightlight in case I get up.

Ellen Marriott (8)
Carfield Primary School, Sheffield

This Is Me

A kennings poem

A positive thinker,
A wheelchair adapter,
A problem solver,
A FND fighter,
A muscle builder,
A big hugger,
A family lover,
A winder upper,
An animal adorer,
A present giver,
A grateful receiver,
A yoga exerciser,
An arts and crafts creator,
A music listener,
A book reader,
A passionate learner,
A comfort seeker,
A meat hater,
A friend maker,
A friend includer,

A confidence builder,
A helpful helper,
A massive supporter,
A big sister,
An amazing daughter,
An inspirational inventor,
A Playmobil store,
A Tiffany doll collector,
A teacher admirer,
A team player,
A hard worker,
A hamster carer,
A dog owner,
A stress fighter,
A huge fidgeter,
A lockdown liker,
A rainbow gazer,
A story writer,
A year six leader,
A secondary school starter,
This is me.

Emily Herbert (11)
Carfield Primary School, Sheffield

Recipe For Poppy

Let's grab a bowl and see what we can make,
And then we'll put it into the oven to bake,
We'll start off with an apple, juicy and green,
It's amazing fuel when you're on the gymnastics team,
I love some fruit twist Fanta,
Though I'm not the one to banter,
Let's add it in, put the bottle in the recycling bin,
The purr of the cutest little kitty cat,
But don't get your fur all over my gymnastics mat,
I hope this cake doesn't turn out floppy,
But just in case, let's add a poppy,
Cake all baked, not floppy at all,
Out comes Poppy all sunburnt and tall.

Poppy Hibberd (10)
Carfield Primary School, Sheffield

Memories

E very day I look back at my strongest memories

R iding over jumps with my favourite horses, Betty and Jack

I sy, Ruby and Kate are great to go on holidays with, especially Greece, Scotland and France

N avigating down the River Spey with my friends

L ying by the fire after stuffing myself with a roast dinner and watching a film with my family

I cing a seven-tiered rainbow cake for my lockdown buddy Lila

L ong walks through the countryside with my friend Bella

Y urt in the woods, and meeting my new kittens, Magic and Daisy.

Erin Grimes (10)
Carfield Primary School, Sheffield

Our Differences

Your voice gives you choice,
No matter how strong,
You should listen to your own,
Personal song.

Sing it bright,
Sing it loud,
Sing it high and touch the clouds.

Sing a song that fights for your rights,
Be kind,
Be caring,
In a world where you are finding your bearings.

Shout across the lands about who you are,
So it can be heard near and far,
Be proud,
Be brave,
Life doesn't have to be grave.

Differences make us who we are,
You just have to believe...

YOU ARE A STAR!

India Bluebell Thackeray (9)
Carfield Primary School, Sheffield

It's All About Me!

M olly is my name and this is about me.

O ne of my favourite things to do is to be with my friends.

L aughing and playing and hoping it will never end.

L iving a happy life is the best thing ever.

Y oung, enjoying good times, wishing it will never end.

I will put my best effort into everything I do in life.

S unny as the sun, I shine even when facing strife.

M y sun might sometimes fade and the clouds roll in.

E ventually, there will be a rainbow and my brightness will win.

Molly Patten (9)

Carfield Primary School, Sheffield

My First Poem

M y name is Maya,

A nd I'm always on fire,

Y ou know this is true because I love learning science,

A nd English, maths, spelling and grammar.

M agic learning is always burning,

A s Mr Thompson is always persuading,

R iding like horses back and forth to the edge of our books,

T o the ends of our pencils,

I always work hard to get the best marks,

N ow I'm standing here at the

E nd of my heart,

Z igzag lines on pages in time.

Maya Martinez (9)
Carfield Primary School, Sheffield

Me

My name is Harley,
I'm seven years old,
My hair is beautiful and shiny,
It's lovely and gold.

I love the colour purple,
My favourite thing is my teddy,
I like spinning around in circles,
And singing ring around the rosy.

My smile is always there,
And I try my best always,
But sometimes I can find it hard,
Because my mind can be in a daze.

I am kind and sweet,
But sometimes I get confused,
I'm not lost or unneat,
My mind is just like a fire.

Harley Donnelly (7)
Carfield Primary School, Sheffield

Me And My Family

Hello everybody, my name is Frankie-Rae,
My favourite thing to do is laugh and play all day,
When I grow up I want to be a star,
And act in plays and films, near and far,
The thing I love the most is my big family,
I am going to tell you about my family tree,
There's my mum, dad and brother,
And my crazy aunties,
And then I have six cousins and they can come in handy,
I like to dance and sing,
And I imagine I have wings,
I could eat apples all day,
And I'm totally cray cray.

Frankie-Rae Watson (7)
Carfield Primary School, Sheffield

Arty Amelie

I'm an arty person,
It makes me fizz inside.
I love to doodle in my books,
It fills me up with pride.
Thousands of ideas clog my mind,
Yet there's more to come.
I squiggle all day and night,
It's so stupendously fun.
I love to do so many things,
Like sketch, paint, colour and draw.
My craft box overflows with stuff,
How could I ever need any more.
My arty world lives inside me,
Like pens inside a drawer.
When I yank it open,
They explode onto the floor.

Amelie Barnett (10)
Carfield Primary School, Sheffield

All About Me

L ouis is my oldest friend, we are the La-Las

A lys is my older sister, funny, annoying and hater of ketchup

W hen I was small I had meningitis, it started from my tummy and travelled to my head

R eading books when I can't get to sleep, overwhelmed but tired, bouncing like a spring

I like thunderstorms when I'm inside, I feel cosy, I am happy

E ating at Hungry Buddha in town on a Saturday fills me with excitement, the flavours dance on my tongue and warm my heart.

Lawrie Gibson (7)

Carfield Primary School, Sheffield

Football

F ootball is the game, I play the game, I dream about it night and day,

O nce I had a fun and fair game,

O nce I had a disappointing game because I got kicked in the leg,

T en-nil win, we helped each other on and cheered till the match was over,

B all at my feet, running as fast as a tiger,

A s the manager pushed us on, we tried our very best to be strong,

L egends of the game, inspire tricks into our spirits,

L ionel beating defenders with ease.

Jake Metcalfe-Skerratt (8)
Carfield Primary School, Sheffield

Little Me

I'm rocking gently in my chair,
Thinking back to when I was a boy,
With emerald eyes and golden hair,
And playing with my favourite toy,
Remembering mud fights with my friend,
Always had a cheeky grin,
My body could stretch and twist and bend,
Playing flames with my violin,
Now I am older and wrinkly and wise,
With still a cheeky look in my emerald eyes,
I still fight with my brother,
I still love eating toffee,
I like being old,
But I miss little me.

Mani Robinson (8)
Carfield Primary School, Sheffield

This Is Me

I have brown eyes and long brown hair,
And every so often I try and dare,
To kick a ball so hard it scores,
And win the match before it pours.

My name is Luna and this poem is mine,
My dad is from Peru,
And I've been there one time.

My name is Luna and this poem is mine,
My mum is from England,
And I think that's just fine,

I am Luna and this poem is mine,
I love my friends,
But I can't think of the last line.

Luna Mendoza (10)
Carfield Primary School, Sheffield

Rainstorm

The rain thrashes down on their gold and ebony
scales,
Their steamy goggles become shining crystals,
Their wings become heavy and drenched as the
sweat on their face is washed away,
By the moons, this is lovely,
The rain is like,
A breath of fresh air,
A cold bath,
An icy drink,
Snowflakes on your tongue,
The taste of mint,
Freckles lift their soaked wings and fly into the
storm,
As they dodge the lightning, they make their way
home.

Alys Gibson (10)
Carfield Primary School, Sheffield

Recipe Of Me

I really love to draw,
My dream in the future is to become a marvellous astronaut,
The things that cheer me up when I'm gloomy,
Are my friends and family,
My happiness raced around me, I was in glee,
One person I admire the most is my mum because she's funny,
And cheers me up when I'm sad,
Built from the stars of the universe and as warm as the embers of the sun,
The ingredients of me are joy, creativity, excitability and fearlessness.

Sonny Woodhead (9)
Carfield Primary School, Sheffield

Who Am I?

Who am I?
Shining like the sun,
Clear blue as the sky,

Friends and family I love,
Reading and swimming too,
I sometimes feel like a dove,
And I could fly up above.

At times I can feel a bit down,
But then I have my friends and my pets,
And they can make me laugh or frown.

Singing, acting and dancing I enjoy,
I save and shop,
To buy a new toy,
So I think this is me,
And I hope you can see.

Erika Payling (9)
Carfield Primary School, Sheffield

18

About Me

My name is Layla and I'm a girl,
I love to dance,
And I can do a good twirl,
I like to laugh and smile,
I'm happy all of the while,
I love the season of autumn,
As leaves go brown and red,
And seeing the sun go down,
I know it's time for bed,
When I was little I used to collect rocks,
My toes feel uncomfy when I wear Crocs,
I like to shout, "Sheesh!"
My dog ran away because I took off its leash.

Layla Lapper (11)
Carfield Primary School, Sheffield

Isabelle's Wish

I can be a little bit nervous like a mouse under a chair,

S ometimes when I'm sad I hug my teddy bear,

A s playful as a kitten with a ball of wool,

B eing a teacher would be really helpful,

E ating chocolate makes me feel happy as I play,

L ovely and warm like a fire on a cold winter's day,

L earning to swim and to speak Spanish,

E sta es mi historia and this is my wish.

Isabelle Jefferies (8)
Carfield Primary School, Sheffield

If Only

Across the fields, I gallop in my dream,
But my dreams are not quite all they seem,
In real life, I ride a variety of horses,
These horses aren't actually designed for courses.

Black, shiny, Friesian horses are my favourite breed,
Instead, I get the worn-out old cob for its walking needs,
I want a supercharged specimen to hit the track,
But instead, I'm still learning this horse riding hack.

Tillie Graham (10)
Carfield Primary School, Sheffield

All About Me

Friends are fantastic, I love gymnastics,
I'm bendy like plastics,
I love gymnastics,
Dancing is my thing,
I do it every day,
I dance when the music starts to play,
On the floor at my gymnastics competition,
I'm going to add a lot of sass just because I am sassy,
My competition is on Saturday so on Friday I'm going to play,
Family cheer me on when I use my superpower, sass.

J'myah Powell (10)
Carfield Primary School, Sheffield

Swimming

S wimming is my favourite sport,

W ater feels refreshing and cool on my bare skin,

I t makes me feel happy and relaxed,

M y body feels strong and flexible like a snake,

M uted sounds in an underwater world beneath the surface,

I see the world in teal blue through my goggles,

N imble legs kick in the water,

G liding through the pool like a dolphin.

Theia Rhodes (7)
Carfield Primary School, Sheffield

It's Just Me

Hello, it's me,
Only me,
Just little old me,
Which me do you see when you see me?
Adventurous me or scaredy-cat me?
Messy me or tidy me?
Maths me or English me?
Chatty me or shy me?
Cuddly me or vicious me?
Encouragable me or stubborn me?
Musical me or silent me?
Playful me or tired me?
You see there are lots of me
That you didn't see.

Iris Desespringalle (8)
Carfield Primary School, Sheffield

Extrordinary Me

M y idol is Sophie Dossie

A cro is my thing

Y ou'll find me at number 87

O nly child but two cousins like sisters

L iverpool is my grandma's home

I nside my head, there are riddles and jokes

V ery big fan of guinea pigs

E specially ones that like to snuggle

R eally really like honeycomb ice cream.

May Oliver (7)
Carfield Primary School, Sheffield

How To Make A Logi Cake

A splash of Star Wars,
A trickle of teddy bears,
A sprinkle of soccer,
Two cups of cheekiness,
Eleven milliliters of Marvel,
A litre of Lego
Four tonnes of family,
Mix in movies,
A whole yoyo,
A gallon of giggles,
Whizz up into a sticky, goopy doughball, squidge it,
Chuck it in the oven for a half-hour,
Take it out and there's your cake.

Logan Barnett (8)
Carfield Primary School, Sheffield

One In A Million

I'm not like everyone else,
I won't follow the crowd, I'm my own crazy self,
I see myself loud and proud,
I'm one in a million, one in a million.

I'm a nature saviour,
Chocolate is my favourite ice cream flavour,
I own a cat and a hamster,
Every day I run faster and faster,
I'm one in a million, one in a million.

Rosie Tyson-Green (9)
Carfield Primary School, Sheffield

Monster

I want to tell a story,
About the monster in my life,
They are only three feet in height,
But they have the most ferocious bite,
When they greet me in the school playground,
My heart begins to pump and pound,
A hug from them will make it right,
At any time of day or night,
So although I am getting bitten,
I will forever be smitten.

Polly Gubbins (9)
Carfield Primary School, Sheffield

About Me

R eally loves cats,

O bviously loves family,

B uilds Lego,

I s a mix of Jamaica and Scotland,

N ot a cheese lover.

M arvellous at maths,

C an't resist food,

N ever without my iPad

A mazing at drawing,

I ncredible at English,

R eally loves chocolate.

Robin McNair (9)

Carfield Primary School, Sheffield

This Is Me

Kind, caring, full of joy,
I'm Ethan and I'm an eight-year-old boy,
I like to play, I like to share,
with my friends,
I'll always be there,
When I grow up, what will I be?
A builder, a cook, an astronaut?
We shall see,
No matter what I do, I'll give it my all,
And always help my friends when they fall.

Ethan Omar-Lyness (8)
Carfield Primary School, Sheffield

Luca - This Is Me

Eyes of blue, hair of brown,
Freckles on the nose,
But never a frown,
Eight years old,
Will never be told,
I think I know best,
And put this to the test,
I send my mum, dad and sister mad,
But I don't mean to be bad,
I drive my hover cart as quick as a flash,
But I drive it so good that I never crash.

Luca Cordon (8)
Carfield Primary School, Sheffield

This Is Me Nothing Changes

This is me,
I have long brown hair,
With light blue eyes,
Nothing changes except my feelings,
I am short and I love football,
The boys say I'm terrible,
I don't listen,
Because this is me, nothing changes,
Everything is marvellous,
Even when I have a bad day,
I love it,
Because this is me.

Lily Rawson (9)
Carfield Primary School, Sheffield

My Favourite Food!

Pasta is nice and so satisfying to eat
I also love hot chocolate, it's milky and sweet
And cold mint ice cream,
As refreshing as a winter morning and cold like
Mount Everest
Dairy Milk chocolate, I like it nice and firm, it snaps
in my mouth
When I chew it I let the flavour run through my
tongue
And then I swallow it.

Max Hodgson (8)
Carfield Primary School, Sheffield

How You Feel

Choices are hard to make,
You hear voices then your anger breaks,
Don't do the wrong thing always the right,
And if you see darkness don't hideaway,
The light will come your way,
So don't be rude, just be nice and play,
Don't hurt others or they'll hurt you,
I do good things and so should you.

Molly McHugh (8)
Carfield Primary School, Sheffield

Canter

As I canter through the fields
It makes me have butterflies in my belly,
It makes me happy and full of joy,
My hands rub on the leather as I grip the reins,
The wind is breezing in my face and it makes me
feel happy,
The horse is getting excited,
I am cantering in the colossal fields,
It makes me feel amazing.

Callie Thomas (7)
Carfield Primary School, Sheffield

What I Like

H appy when I see Arthur my dog
A rthur is my best friend
R ed and blue are my favourite colours
R ain makes me mad
I ndoraptor is a dinosaur
S heep in Minecraft are fluffy and funny
O reos are my favourite biscuit
N anna lives with me and my mummy.

Harrison Davidson (7)
Carfield Primary School, Sheffield

Guess Who I Am

I like to read,
I like to write,
I like the speed,
Who am I?
I like to scooter,
I like to fly,
I love the computer,
Who am I?
I have blonde hair,
I have blue eyes,
Are you aware?
Who am I?
Starts with J ends with an,
Believe me, one day, I will visit Japan.

Julian De Morais (7)
Carfield Primary School, Sheffield

My Name Is Ella

My name is Ella,
I am eight,
I like to dance,
And roller skate,
My hair is brown,
My eyes are blue,
With a bit of brown,
Which is really cool,
At school I enjoy maths,
My teacher makes me laugh,
I shine bright like the sun,
When playing with friends, having fun.

Ella Gudgeon (8)
Carfield Primary School, Sheffield

I Am Me

I am me,
But I don't live in a tree,
I am silly,
But my name is not Billy,
My glasses are blue,
But they are not stuck on with glue,
My favourite food is pizza with cheese,
But never with mushy peas,
I have a pet hamster, Popcorn,
Who wakes me up at the crack of dawn.

Zac Rodway (9)
Carfield Primary School, Sheffield

Holiday

H olidays are the best,
O ver are all the tests,
L ove to the ones who are upset,
I look forward to the feast,
D addy eats like a beast,
A t the end, it's time to reminisce,
Y our days that were bliss,
S ummer is finally over.

Rafia Noor (8)

Carfield Primary School, Sheffield

This Is Me

D is for dreamy because I like to dream
A is for awesome, that's in my bloodstream
S is for smart, I like to read a lot
T is for talkative, that's what I got
A is for amazing, my parents tell me so
N is for naughty, why I don't know.

Dastan Rosario Spinola (7)
Carfield Primary School, Sheffield

I Love Nature

I love nature,
I love the birds,
I like how they tweet,
I like now nature slithers along the ground,
Thank you for the worms, that help to give us food,
Thank you to the bees for pollinating the flowers,
I love all the nature that is in this world,
It makes me feel happy.

Ayla Adams (7)
Carfield Primary School, Sheffield

Umair The Athlete

I am like a ball of fun, bouncy and round,
As fast as a cheetah and as cool as a cucumber,
When I get angry I am as furious as a rapid bull,
Feeling miserable, no problem, a game of Roblox
will cheer you up
My family is the best,
Carry on your day and I'll have some fun hooray!

Umair Khan (8)
Carfield Primary School, Sheffield

The Is Me

Violets are blue,
Roses are red,
So is the hair
growing out of my head!

I like a good hug,
all up snug.
I'm sometimes shy
but I don't know why.

I am quite fast
but I can't run past
a packet of sweets
or tasty treats!

Eloise Meadows (8)
Carfield Primary School, Sheffield

My Chicken

C oconut is my chicken

O h how cute she is

C hicken friends are Hedwig and Peanut

O range for her beak

N ut-brown feathers sticking out

U nder my arm, I cuddle her

T ick-tock, the time passes by but I always get to say hi!

Morla Fabian (7)
Carfield Primary School, Sheffield

Football

H appy is what I like to be,
A nd playing football is important to me,
Y esterday I played for my team,
D ez is our coach and he leads our dream,
E very day I play football with my friends,
N ever stop playing and the fun never ends.

Hayden Hales (10)
Carfield Primary School, Sheffield

Me

This is a poem about me,
I love to dance and swim in the sea,
When the school bell has gone,
The park is the best place to go,
There's always a friend there I know,
We go on the swings, climb on the frame,
And play hide-and-seek, my favourite game.

Sophia Fearnley (8)
Carfield Primary School, Sheffield

Art

A lways drawing in my

R oom, that's where I'll be,

T rying new ideas,

I nky fingers,

S elf-tattooing,

T hey are temporary though,

I 'm underage,

C an't wait to get a real one done!

Nancy Tonks (10)

Carfield Primary School, Sheffield

My Poem

Hi my name is Grace,
And my mummy says,
I have a beautiful little face,
I love going to school and being with all my friends,
Also happy when the school days ends,
When I go home I play with my dog, we like to watch TV,
And he lies on my knee.

Grace Fearnley (7)
Carfield Primary School, Sheffield

This Is Me This Is You

This is me, this is you
We are one as a pair
Together we are two and we like to share
Then we have fun and like to dance
When we are one, we go into a trance
When we are apart, I want to go back to the start
So that we both get another chance.

Tabitha Rose Williams (7)
Carfield Primary School, Sheffield

Things That I Like

E lliot is a very kind boy,

L ike a funny monkey who brings joy,

L ikes playing in the yard,

I always try really hard,

O ften Elliot loves a cuddle with his brother,

T otally like a koala hugging its mother.

Elliot Baldwin-Dial (7)

Carfield Primary School, Sheffield

I Am Saif

S mart and super, I always do my homework,

A rtistic and amazing, I'm a talented illustrator,

I maginative and intelligent, I step into the story when I rule,

F unny and friendly, I make all my friends laugh.

Saif Khan (10)
Carfield Primary School, Sheffield

The Boy With Confidence

Sometimes I am confident,
Sometimes I am shy,
Sometimes I am brave,
Sometimes I am sad,
But I am always helpful and kind,
Sometimes I am fine,
And sometimes I am not in the mood,
But I am always helpful and kind.

Jacob Harrop (8)
Carfield Primary School, Sheffield

I Am

I am me,
I am creative,
I am inventive,
I am an animal lover,
I am a good brother,
I am me.

I will be,
A Lego master,
Building faster,
A great inventor,
In a science centre,
I will be!

Joseph Ward (10)
Carfield Primary School, Sheffield

This Is Me

This is me, I like to sing made-up songs and do art,
This is me, I like to see family and friends,
This is me, I like video games and Lego,
This is me, I like games and fun,
This is me, I like imagination and playfights.

Oliver Morgan (8)
Carfield Primary School, Sheffield

Unique Ugonna

U nique, always going to be special,
G enerous, always giving,
O riginal, with innovative ideas,
N ice and caring,
N oble, always honourable,
A ffectionate, a delight to know.

Ugonna Onyemaucheya (10)

Carfield Primary School, Sheffield

This Is Yasmin

Y asmin shines like the sun

A nd she is bright and fun

S he lends a helping hand

M aking people feel grand

I deas pop into her head

N ow she's going off to bed.

Yasmin Lindsay (7)
Carfield Primary School, Sheffield

Me

I am Rudi
Red and blue are my favourite colours
How about you?
I like Lego
Batman too
I really like going to the zoo
Lions, tigers, hippos and snakes
On my birthday I like to eat cakes.

Rudi Ellis (7)
Carfield Primary School, Sheffield

This Is Me

C aring, cat-loving Connie,
O ften eats oaty biscuits,
N early always singing and dancing,
N ever stops playing,
I nto the future,
E xciting things await.

Connie Czauderna-Naylor (7)

Carfield Primary School, Sheffield

A Recipe For Me

Three tablespoons of kindness,
A pinch of humour,
A slice of confidence,
Two hundred grams of smartness,
A cup of thoughtfulness,
And a sprinkle of fun,
That's how you make me.

Benjamin Holmes (9)
Carfield Primary School, Sheffield

This Is Me

A kennings poem

Who is it?
Super drawer
Cola drinker,
Game player,
Bike rider,
Dog lover,
Seed planter,
Lego builder,
Book reader,
Kind brother,
Guess who?

Aubrey Doherty (8)
Carfield Primary School, Sheffield

Me

I do three things in a row,
Karate, acrobatics and swimming,
I'm as busy as a fast car,
My voice may sound different,
But I'm as special as the moon.

Harri Quinlen (8)
Carfield Primary School, Sheffield

All About Me

A kennings poem

Maths lover
Ball kicker
Hard worker
Pet lover
Spider despiser
Question solver
Sun admirer
Rain hater
PE liker
Kennings creator!

Mathew Zachariah (10)

Carfield Primary School, Sheffield

Splits

Every day I love to stretch,
I practise the splits after school,
I make a list,
I tick things off,
If I don't get to practice,
I feel lost.

Roma M (10)
Carfield Primary School, Sheffield

The Roscoe Poem

My name is Roscoe,
I'm nearly eight years old,
When I'm happy I jump up and down,
And when I'm sad I lower my head down.

Roscoe Ferraby (7)
Carfield Primary School, Sheffield

Me

I hate being angry,
Put it in the bin,
I feel better,
When happiness comes in.

Arthur Werner (8)
Carfield Primary School, Sheffield

This Is Me

I love my dog, she always hugs you,
I love to have family nights where we watch a film
and have some snacks,
Running, jumping, exercising, fit and healthy all for
myself,
I'm an animal lover, have lots of pets,
Hug them, kiss them everywhere,
My favourite sport is gymnastics, front flips,
backflips, splits, practising
every day, trying to be a professional,
My family is the most important to me because
they're always there for me,
Me, me, this is me, love animals and family.

Kacey Bainbridge (9)
Even Swindon Primary School, Raybrook Park

It's All About Me

My name is Jenson Bird, but sadly I don't fly,
But mum always says if I believe, I can touch the sky
I am definitely different, very funny, I will make you cry
I sometimes struggle with my workload, but nevertheless, I don't give up, I try
I love all things history, music and space
Ask me some questions, I know loads about the human race
In my spare time I do performing arts, I sing and dance and act
I have even performed live on stage, no jokes, that is a fact
My little sister Raeya, she's cute, but don't be fooled
She is the troublemaker, and the one to break the rules
My mum is my best friend, I love her lots and lots
I also love my dad, even when he does smelly pops
As you can see I'm happy, I am an all-round good guy who is sometimes misunderstood,

All I ask is that you take a second, don't judge this book, get to know me, if you would.

Jenson Bird (9)

Even Swindon Primary School, Raybrook Park

All About Me

My name is Erin Giles,
My favourite gymnast is Simone Biles,
I can run for a few miles,
I've got a lot of strange smiles,
I'm ten years of age,
And I'm still not allowed a Facebook page,
Wasps I don't like,
My lovely dad is called Mike,
I love climbing trees,
But I usually graze my knees,
My favourite animal is a panda,
When I do flips I'm a very good lander,
That practically sums up me,
I better stop this now, I need to have my tea.

Erin Giles (10)
Even Swindon Primary School, Raybrook Park

Me

I am a star on a football field,
Passing and striking, racing and chasing,
I'm a keen learner, maths is my favourite,
I'm as good as gold,
I shine like a star,
My parents love me,
Why wouldn't anyone,
This is my life,
I do as I please,
I am an angel, sweet and cute,
This is me, this is me,
I'm very skinny,
I don't like my food, most people would assume,
I like the way I am though,
This is me, this is me.

Dawson Handy (10)
Even Swindon Primary School, Raybrook Park

What Makes Me

W eirdly wonderful little girl,
H armlessly going about daily life,
A ctively working hard to be my best,
T he best friend ever.

M indful which keeps me calm,
A rtistic and creative,
K ind-hearted and gentle,
E nergetically constantly jumping around,
S mart and sassy.

M eticulous in my work,
E dgy, I like to keep on trend.

Jessica Robertson (10)
Even Swindon Primary School, Raybrook Park

This Is Me

T his is me, running up the wing fast,
H ow are you so fast, some people may ask,
I magine me being a football star,
S ome people say I may achieve it.

I love my iPad and my parents too,
S omeday I wish to see a kangaroo.

M y football career has gone well so far,
E ver since I've started I have always played as a striker!

Finley Griffin (9)

Even Swindon Primary School, Raybrook Park

This Is Me

This is me, blonde hair, blue eyes and especially
small thighs,
Size two in shoes, don't mind if I lose,
Smart and fit, this poem is lit,
Lots of hopes and dreams,
Hopes and wishes,
This is me and you can't change it,
I like to game, this poem isn't lame,
You can't change me,
This is me,
I am who I am,
I can act as I want,
This is me, this me.

Lilly Smith (9)
Even Swindon Primary School, Raybrook Park

This Is Me

T his is me, this is me,

H ow funny I am, you will see,

I love going to the swimming pool,

S ports are my favourite, especially football.

I play at the back in football, also known as defence,

S hooting at the goal is not where I play best.

M y life is incredibly cool,

E very sweet in the world makes me drool.

Jack Griffin (9)

Even Swindon Primary School, Raybrook Park

Roses

Roses are red, violets are blue,
Playing games makes me think of you,
Playing football is what I do,
Making me think of you or feeling blue
At school, I may be naughty but I try,
My best friend Carol helps me a lot,
I see funny Jen to help me with my thoughts
My mum said you or others might win,
but always try my best as this is me.

Iziyah Windslow-Davis (7)
Even Swindon Primary School, Raybrook Park

All About Me

T he trophy is my thing, winning as well,
H elping animals and my classmates too,
I ntelligent I am, leaving is my thing,
S mart I am and craziness I have,

I nternet I know a lot,
S nakes I am not afraid of them, brave I am,

M other and Father I love,
E lephants I love.

Aarohi Singh (8)
Even Swindon Primary School, Raybrook Park

This Is Me And You Cannot Change That

I have a good personality and I can write
fantastically,
I have shiny hair and my mum says I'm a bit of a
mare,
Size 3.5 in shoes and I don't like zoos,
You can't change me,
I am who I am,
I'm a fast runner,
Especially in the summer,
I have nice green hazel eyes,
So please let me win this prize.

Jools McMahon (9)

Even Swindon Primary School, Raybrook Park

This Is Me

T urquoise is my favourite colour,
H orses are my favourite animal,
I like spicy stuff,
S weets, I don't like,

I like Minecraft, it's my favourite,
S easide is a lovely place to go on holiday,

M aths is my favourite subject,
E vie is my name.

Evie Wischhusen (9)

Even Swindon Primary School, Raybrook Park

This Is Me

H orse riding is a dangerous sport,
O r a fun sport,
R iding around I am,
S addles, I sit in,
E vie rides,

R ides around,
I n the stable for ages,
D ressage and jumping,
I magine the course,
N ancing about,
G rowing ponies.

Evie Amelia Adkin (10)
Even Swindon Primary School, Raybrook Park

Gymnastics

G ymnastics are the best,

Y ou hardly get any rest,

M edals and trophies,

N ew routines,

A ccidents but not always,

S pecial moves,

T his is me,

I n good pain when you do you're best,

C ompetitions and clapping,

S plits and enjoying.

Jaida Aldridge (10)
Even Swindon Primary School, Raybrook Park

This Is Me Actual Me

I am the greatest showgirl you can ever meet,
I am as strong as a tiger that gnaws on your feet,
What do you know,
I like the greatest show,
I sing louder,
I follow my power,
I listen to my heart,
Where will I go to?
Do I fix or do I see?
I like to dance and boogie and prance,
This is me!

Olivia Blewett

Even Swindon Primary School, Raybrook Park

Caleigh

C rafting is a hobby,

A nd reading is a part of my life,

L aw is what I want to learn,

E ngland is where I live,

I nspiration is a thing I look up to,

G iving up is not my thing,

H aving friends and family around me is like knowing people are there for me.

Caleigh Marques (10)

Even Swindon Primary School, Raybrook Park

This Is All About Me

T hea is my name,

H arley is my devil sister,

I love my family,

S chool is fun, PE is my favourite,

I am my mum's firstborn child,

S ome people say I look like my mummy,

M iss Wood is my teacher,

E den is my best friend.

Thea Elisha (10)

Even Swindon Primary School, Raybrook Park

This Is Me

My eye colour is green,
My favourite colour is pink,
I love being kind,
And helping my friends,
I love my dog,
She's really cool,
My favourite sport is tennis,
I hope to become a singer,
Most people say I'm good,
One day I wish to see a kangaroo,
And that is me.

Valentina Tarosso (9)
Even Swindon Primary School, Raybrook Park

The Girl

The girl who has brown hair,
The name starts with an A,
The girl loves sporting,
Every time you're upset come to the girl,
The second letter in her name is R,
You can count on me anytime, just call me,
I love you with all my heart,
I have five letters in my name and five siblings.

Ariel Kernse (10)
Even Swindon Primary School, Raybrook Park

This Is Me

This is me, this is me,
How good I am, you will see,
I used to be a keeper but now I'm a right-winger,
I played against Strattons and scored a thrashing goal,
I play on my trampoline and do 360s,
My favourite food is ham, egg and chips,
I eat it all up and slurp with my lips.

Charlie Edwards (9)
Even Swindon Primary School, Raybrook Park

This Is Me

My name is Maxi
I don't pay the taxi
I am very gamey
I have a friend named Jamie
She's not very brainy
I have shiny teeth
This poem is very rhymey
I don't like pudding because it's so slimy
I'm never late to school
Or I'd be a fool

Maxi S (9)
Even Swindon Primary School, Raybrook Park

Just Me!

I'm as sweet as a fairy,
And as sensitive as a kitten.

My mind is always learning,
I do not find it concerning.

I love my friends and family,
I adore them very much.

My home is my safe place,
And I love giving huge hugs.

Ziya Rose (9)
Even Swindon Primary School, Raybrook Park

The Me! Wrap

I'm scared of a spider, and I'm a bike rider,
I like my cats and my hats,
I love my switch and being on a golf pitch,
I hate running,
But I like jumping,
My favourite food is curry and I'm never in a hurry,
I also like tea and this is me.

Jennie Campbell (9)
Even Swindon Primary School, Raybrook Park

Bethany

B eautiful like a butterfly,

E xtraordinary like a star,

T ough like a lion,

H ave a growth mindset then you won't give up,

A mazing like an astronaut,

N o giving up now,

Y ou are who you want to be.

Bethany Scott (9)

Even Swindon Primary School, Raybrook Park

That Is Me

I am an animal lover,
I love chocolate,
I have a movie night every Friday,
It is the best,
I love school,
Maths is my favourite subject,
My dog is so fluffy,
It is so cute,
I love cats and dogs,
Animals are so cute.

Jamie-Lee Tewkesbury (9)
Even Swindon Primary School, Raybrook Park

Gym Dog

G ym dog flips and flies until he dies,

Y ou would never miss him,

M edals and trophies are his life,

D oing his very best,

O r failing at the very best,

G oing to competitions is the best.

Amelia Francis (10)

Even Swindon Primary School, Raybrook Park

This Is Me

Hi my name is Layla
I like to write books
And sometimes I write comics
I hope to be able to make a paper aeroplane
I hope to throw it further than the last plane
So I hope you like what I wrote about myself.

Layla Matthews (10)
Even Swindon Primary School, Raybrook Park

This Is Me Like Me

I like to jump, I like to learn,
You will see what I am,
I do dances, I do mimes,
This is a rhyme,
If you see my friends are here,
One of them will see,
What they are,
This is me,
How I am!

Peri Ekiz (10)
Even Swindon Primary School, Raybrook Park

Krisha

K indness is my middle name,

R eady to play any game,

I ntelligent but sometimes silly,

S miling and always funny,

H appy to help others,

A mazing is my nature.

Krisha Sunar (9)

Even Swindon Primary School, Raybrook Park

My Hamster Mikey

M arvellously mischievous

I ncredibly greedy

K indly shows love with his cuddles

E xtremely energetic (when he's not sleeping)

Y ou can't help but love him.

Mason Ferguson (9)

Even Swindon Primary School, Raybrook Park

About Me

E lephants are one of my favourite animals,
T ennis is my favourite sport,
H anging out with my friends makes me happy,
A nd I love dogs,
N aughtiness is my hobby.

Ethan Marques (7)

Even Swindon Primary School, Raybrook Park

Me

Brown eyes like chocolate,
As sweet as a lolly,
As kind as a butterfly,
Excellent like ice cream,
Funny like a parrot,
And pretty like a button.

Layla Cousens (9)
Even Swindon Primary School, Raybrook Park

This Is Me

I have strawberry-blonde hair,
My favourite animal is a horse,
Blue eyes,
I am tall,
Doesn't matter if I lose,
I love this rap.

Ollie Loveridge (9)
Even Swindon Primary School, Raybrook Park

Halloween

Halloween is my favourite holiday
I like it because it's spooky
The weather is crackling
And the waves are crashing.

Jessica Jacobson (7)
Even Swindon Primary School, Raybrook Park

The Kajetan Rap

You may think I'm smart, you may think I'm stupid,
You may think I'm crafty, but I've got nothing to do with it.
But hold on to your seatbelts 'cause I'm gonna floor it!
Bam, ram, slam bam tram!
I'm giving you all the Kajetan rap.
(Rap rap rap)

I was born on the 24th of September,
I don't even wanna remember.
Oh gosh, that awful day,
Gosh, I thought I was a stray.
There I was, so alone,
Nobody to call on my fetus phone.
I was in my mother practising karate,
Yay, I was having a party!
Kicking about, not a care in the world,
And then I felt a sudden whirl!

"One more push Ms Jowsa and you'll see his knee."
I'm telling you this, it surprised me.
I wailed out in tears, "How'd you know I'm a he?"
The midwife shouted, "Oh lord, he can speak!"
I added on, "Do you want a speech?"
I thrived and I drove through the night,
Bam, ram, slam bam tram!
I'm giving you all the Kajetan rap!

When I was one I flew into space,
When I was two I caught a suitcase.
When I was three I was stung by a bee,
When I was four I grew a tree.
When I was five, I swam the Pacific,
When I was six, I was told to be specific.
When I was seven, I robbed a bank with my sister,
When I was eight I was caught by the prime
minister.
When I was nine I was an actor in a manor,
When I was ten, I was a computer programmer.

So that's what I am, so that's what I'll be,
With a K, with an A,
With a J, with an E,
With a T, with an A,
With an N.
So that's what I am, so that's what I'll be,
Mr Kajetan, Mr Krajewski, Mr Me.
Bam, ram, slam bam tram,
I'm giving you all the Kajetan Krajewski rap!

Kajetan Krajewski (10)

Ferndale Primary School, Great Barr

This Is Me

Ya may think I'm happy
Ya may think I'm sad
Ya may think I'm crazy
Ya may think I'm mad
Hold your horses, listen to me
Let me tell you a little something about me
A hip, a hop, a hip hop hap
I'm giving you the Daisy Price rap

When I was one I could walk
When I was two I ate some chalk
When I was three I became poor
When I was four I knocked my mom's door
When I was five I ate a beehive
When I was six I dived
When I was seven I ate my mom's dog
When I was eight I stepped on a ginormous log
When I was nine I brought a pen
When I was ten I laid a hen

I am giving you all the Daisy Price rap.

Daisy Price (11)
Ferndale Primary School, Great Barr

The D-J-B Rap

Ya may think I'm funny, you may think I'm rad,
Ya may think I'm weird, you may think I'm bad.
But hang on to your horses, so make sure you're
ready,
Ensuring that none of you aren't too steady.
A bip, a bop, a bip bop bap!
I'm giving you all the D-J-B rap!

I was born on the 4th of July,
It was midnight, I was pretty sly.
I was in my mother, bunched up tight,
When the doctors saw the most magnificent sight.
But when my head popped out I didn't wanna
leave,
Though I was so happy, I could finally breathe.

Then I heard some people give a shout,
"One push Mrs Johnson, and she'll be out!"
Well, that was weird, they called me a "she"
I mean at least I'm not really a he.
When the doctor shouted, "Come on, one more
squeeze!"
But unfortunately for my mom, that wasn't a
breeze.

But thankfully I finally came out,
When my mom gave a thankful pout.
A bip, a bop, a bip bop bap!
I'm giving you all the D-J-B rap!

When I was one I was really lazy,
When I was two I crawled around like crazy.
When I was three, I did a big smelly poopy,
When I was four I sent my mom loopy.
When I was five, I started primary school,
When I was six, I was really rad and cool.
When I was seven I went to the beach,
When I was eight, I ate a juicy peach.
When I was nine I got my first pet,
When I was ten, I got the ball in the net.

So that's what I am, that's what I'll be.

With a D, with an R,
With a C, with a Y.
So that's what I am, that's what I'll be.
Miss D'rcy, Miss Johnson,
Miss Daughter, Miss Me.

A bip, a bop, a bip bop bap!
I'm giving you all the D-J-B rap!

D'rcy Johnson-Bryan (10)

Ferndale Primary School, Great Barr

The Peter Reter Rap

Yo listen to this beat
I'm gonna spend the beat
You might as well listen, I'm turning up the heat

When I was one I fell into a ditch
When I was two I became rich
When I was three I got some bars
When I was four I went to Mars
When I was five I went to Jupiter
When I was six I got less stupider
When I was seven I baked a cake
When I was eight I went to a lake
When I was nine I got a rhyme
When I was ten I got a dime

Year so that is me, that's who I'll be
What a show I put in low
Yeah, so that's the Peter Reter rap yo.

Peter Vassilev (10)
Ferndale Primary School, Great Barr

This Is Me, Karanvir

You may think I'm bright, you may think I'm dark,
You may think I'm silly, you may think I spark.
But hang on to your seats and listen right now,
I'm gonna tell you something that'll make you bow.
A hip, a hop, a hip hop hap,
I'm giving you all the Karanvir Singh rap.

I was born on the 13th of August,
I remember that flawless day.
I was reflecting in my mother's eyes,
Life was good but it was full of lies.
Though I was blind as a bat,
I tried to hit a six but I got scratched by a cat.

I was crying I wanted to leave,
But I could barely breathe.
Then I hear some people give a shout,
"His nose is bleeding,"
Then I passed out.
Woke up again in the hospital and said, "How'd you know I'm a he?"
Doctor said, "Oh good lord he can talk,"

I jumped out of the bed and said, "Now watch me walk."
I jooked and jived around that room,
Balam bam boolah, balam ba diddy boom.
A hip, a hop, a hip hop hap,
I'm giving you all the Karanvir Singh rap.

When I was one I got hit by a bat,
When I was two I wore the magician's hat.
When I was three I got locked in a machine,
When I was four, I had an awful dream.
When I was five I played the flute,
When I was six, I robbed a bank with good loot.
When I was seven I started getting thinner,
When I was eight I ate the dog's dinner.
When I was nine I travelled the world,
When I was ten, I hurled.
So that's what I am, that's what I'll be.
With a K, with an A, with an R.
So that's what I am, that's what I'll be,
Mr Kar, Mr Kav, Mr Singh, Mr Me.

A hip, a hop, a hip hop hap,
I'm giving you all the Karanvir Singh rap.

Karanvir Singh (10)

Ferndale Primary School, Great Barr

My Daring Inspirer

A young fighter,
A courageous comeback,
A sharer,
A glory hunter,
An inspirer,
A community helper,
A racket smasher,
A fierce forehand,
A limit pusher,
A passionate player,
A brilliant backhand,
A record-breaker,
Who am I?
Emma Raducanu.

Abeera Khan (10)
Ferndale Primary School, Great Barr

I Am Who I Am!

Ya may think I'm funny, ya may think I'm mad,
Ya may think I'm crazy or you may think I'm bad.
But hold on to your whiskers,
I'll relax your brain,
But don't worry, it won't drive you insane.
I give you the Evie (rap, rap, rap)

I was born on the 23rd of May,
I remember very well that horrendous day.
I was in my mama snuggled up tight,
My poor old mama must have had a fright.
Living freely, no worries on my mind,
I was so happy,
Might as well call me happy Larry.

Then I hear someone give a shout,
"One more push Mrs Smith and she'll be out!"
I'm telling that really questioned me,
I shouted out, "Hey! How do you know I'm a she?"
Midwife shouted, "Omg she can speak!"
I popped my head out and said, "Now watch me
weep."

Like there's nothing to see,
I danced and pranced around that room,
Salam dam diddy diddy boom pat pap.

When I was one I crawled around the chairs,
When I was two I ate all the pears.
When I was three I started writing,
When I was four life became more exciting.
When I was five I went to school,
When I was six I could finally swim in a pool.
When I was seven I burnt all four fingers,
When I was eight I joined a chain of singers.
When I was nine I became a climber,
When I was ten I became a fashion designer.

So that's what I am,
And that's what I'll be.
With an E,
With a V,
With an I,
With an E.
So that's what I am,
And that's what I'll be.

Miss Evie,
Miss Smith,
Just me.
Pit pat, pit pit-pat,
I'm giving you all the Evie rap (rap, rap, rap).

Evie Smith (10)
Ferndale Primary School, Great Barr

The Shivam Rap

A kennings poem

Pro gamer,
Top winner,
Greedy eater,
Talented footballer,
Fast runner,
Girl footballer,
Wolf lover,
Heart breaker,
Professional drawer,
Loving sister,
Daydreamer,
Caring daughter,
Funny joker,
Guess who I am...
I am Shivam!

Shivam Thakur (11)
Ferndale Primary School, Great Barr

This Is Me

You may think I'm light, you may think I'm smart,
You may think I'm bright, you may think I'm dark.

But hang on to your seats and listen right here,
I'm going to tell you something that will itch your ear,
A hip, a pop, a hip-pop nap,
I'm giving you all the Roman Banga rap (rap, rap, rap).

I was born on the 30th of July, I remember that magnificent moment,
I was in my mom curled up tight,
But I have to say it was dark as night,
I have to say I didn't want to leave,
I was so moody I didn't want to sleep!
Then I heard someone shout,
"So close Mrs Banga and he'll be out"
That was confusing for me,
"How do you know I'm a he?"
The doctor shouted, "My goodness he can talk!"
My head got squeezed out and I said "Watch me talk"

"Balam bam boolah, balam ba diddy boom"
A hip, a pop, a hip-pop blatt,
I'm giving you all the Roman Banga rap (rap, rap, rap).

When I was one I sat on grass,
When I was two I had a very itchy rash,
When I was three I started getting thinner,
When I was four I ate the dog's dinner,
When I was five I learnt how to drive,
When I was six I swallowed a hard drive,
When I was seven I dreamt of heaven,
When I was eight I had loads of fate,
When I was nine I had a fat mate,
When I was ten I slapped a fat hen.

So that's what I am and that's what I'll be,
With an R with an O, with an M with an A, with an N,
So that's what I am and that's what I'll be,
Mr Ro, Mr Roman,
Mr Banga, Mr Me.

A hip, a pop, a hip pop pat,
I'm giving you all the Roman Banga rap (rap, rap, rap).

Roman Banga (10)

Ferndale Primary School, Great Barr

This Is Me

A kennings poem

Peaceful pet lover
Roblox ruler
Independent reader
Fabulous dancer
Dream maker
Master builder
Doughnut hater
Dazzling sister
Soulmate sister
Partner parents
Kitty in crime
Love in mind
Charming me
Loving me
This is me!

Olivia Arblaster (10)
Ferndale Primary School, Great Barr

Daawud Rassool Rap

You may think I'm clever, you may think I have
heart,
You may think I'm crazy, you may think I'm smart.
But hang on to your books,
I will build all of your dreams,
I'm telling you, it's not what it seems.
Dip, bop, dip bip dap!
I'm giving you the Rassool's rap!

I was born on the 25th of March,
Being so hyper, I felt very parched.
I was in my mother, bunched up tight,
Swimming around, I felt very light.
My mother was screaming, she was really scared,
I was so happy, always prepared.

Then I heard some people give a shout,
"One push Mrs Rassool and he'll be out!"
I'm telling you, that was a puzzle to me,
I shouted out, "How'd you know I'm a he?"
The midwife said, "This is magnificent, he can
speak!"

I popped out my head and said, "Want a speech!?"
I talked and chattered all day long,
Bong, dong, bang, bing, ding bing bong!
Dip, bob, dip bip dap!
I'm giving you the Rassool's rap!

When I was one I went to the zoo,
When I was two I knew how to say boo!
When I was three I played with my brother,
When I was four, I got another.
When I was five I went to Alton Towers,
When I was six, I watched Clutch Powers.
When I was seven, I had a hoard,
When I was eight, I went abroad.
When I was nine I tied my lace,
When I was ten, I went to space.

So that's what I am, that's what I'll be.
With a D, with an AA,
With a W, with a UD,
So that's what I am, that's what I'll be.
Mr Daawud, Mr Rassool,
Mr Brother, Just me.

A dip, bop, dip bip dap,
I'm giving you the Rassool's rap!

Daawud Rassool (10)

Ferndale Primary School, Great Barr

I Am...

A kennings poem

A loyal believer,
A fearless fighter,
An honest helper,
An optimistic sister,
An ambitious youngster,
A wise friendship maker,
A dedicated environment carer,
An animal lover,
A humble book reader.
Put these together...
I am Umayrah!

Umayrah Rahman (10)
Ferndale Primary School, Great Barr

This Is Me

You may think I'm bright, you may think I'm dull.
You may think I'm nice, you may think I'm dumb.
But hang on to your seats and listen right here,
I'm gonna tell you something that will burst you
into laughing tears.
A hip a hop, a hip hop hap,
I'm giving you all the Louie Roberts rap.

I was born on the 2nd of March,
I was royalty, all the doctors prepared me an arch.
I was royal, I was the best in town,
It was like that until my brother came around,
As soon as he was around,
Every night I heard the same sound,
"Waa waa!" that's the only sound I ever heard.
It sounded like a baby deer that lost its herd,
I came downstairs and said, "I should be loved
too."
They took one look and said, "That's all we do."
I started saying "I'm just as cool."
"We're not comparing you but he still drools."

A hip hop, a hip hop hap,
I'm giving you all the Louie Roberts rap.

When I was one I bathed in the sink,
When I was two I really loved pink,
When I was three I was the victor,
When I was four I started drawing pictures,
When I was five, my brother was alive,
When I was six I learnt a few tricks,
When I was seven my cousin was eleven,
When I was eight, say goodbye to Devon,
When I was nine school got harder,
When I was 10 I had a lesson with Mrs Harders.

So that's who I am, that's who I'll stay,
With an L with an O,
With a U, with an I and with an E,
That's who I am and that's who I'll be.
Mr Louie, Mr Jay, Mr Roberts, Mr Me,
A hip a hop, a hip hop hap,
I'm giving you all the Louie Roberts rap.

Louie Roberts (10)
Ferndale Primary School, Great Barr

The Logan Heard Rap

You may think I'm funny, you may think I'm sad,
But underneath my layers, you know I'm really rad.
So hold on to your head and hold onto your brain,
Because I'm about to send in the Logan Heard
train.
Bip, bop, bip bop bang!
I'm giving you all the Logan Heard rap.

I was born on the 11th of November,
Being too young then, I don't remember.
I was in my mother, all curled up nice,
She was probably shaking, like a bag of rice.
Roaming around freely, no thought in my head,
No way I was stiff, like toasted bread.

Then I heard some people give the word,
"One more push and he'll be out Mrs Heard."
I tried to say, that was hard for me,
But when I spoke, it was like a buzz from a bee.
Doctor said, "Look you have a son,
He'll play all day, won't that be fun."

A bip, bop, bip bop bang!
I'm giving you the Logan Heard rap (rap, rap, rap)

When I was one, I went a bit loopy,
When I was two, I did my first poopy.
When I was three, I did my first drawing,
When I was four, I heard my dad snoring.
When I was five, I was quite the dancer,
When I was six, I battled cancer.
When I was seven, I went to some parties,
When I was eight, I ate a bag of Smarties.
When I was nine, I flew like a bird,
When I was ten, I was King Logan Heard.
So that's what I am, that's what I'll be.
With an L, with an O,
With a G, with an Λ,
With an N.

So that's what I am, that's what I'll be,
Mr Logan, Mr Brother,
Mr Heard, Mr Me.
Bip, bop, bip bop bang!
I'm giving you all the Logan Heard rap (rap, rap, rap).

Logan Heard (11)
Ferndale Primary School, Great Barr

The Leela Harrison Rap

You may think I'm funny, you may think I'm bad,
You may think I'm crazy, you may think I'm rad.
But hang on to your dogs, I will make you happy,
After all, I am a bit sassy.
A beep a boop, a beep boop bap,
This is the Leela Harrison rap!

I was born on the 16th of Feb,
I was so happy, I was protected by a web.
I was in my mother, curled up tight,
My poor old mother must have had a fright!
Floating around freely, no worries on my mind,
I felt so good, I knew I was gonna be kind.

Then I heard some people shout,
"One push Mrs Harrison and she'll be out!"
I'm telling you, that was a puzzle to me,
I shouted out, "How's you know I'm a she?"
The midwife shouted, "Good lord she can talk!"
I popped out my head and said, "Watch me walk!"
Balam boolah bam, balam a biddy boom,

A beep, a boop, a beep boop bap,
This is the Leela Harrison rap!

When I was one, I punched my sister,
When I was two, I stood on my uncle's blister.
When I was three I started getting thinner,
When I was four, I made my own dinner.
When I was five I joined reception,
When I was six, I showed I'm an exception.
When I was seven, I rode my bike,
When I was eight, I went on my first hike.
When I was nine I got a new mattress,
When I was ten I became an actress!

So that's what I am and that's what I'll be,
With an L, with an E,
With an E, L, A.
So that's what I am and I'll be okay,
Miss Leela, Miss Harrison,
Miss Sister, Miss Me.
A beep a boop, a beep boop bap,
This is the Leela Harrison rap!

Leela Harrison (10)
Ferndale Primary School, Great Barr

Weerasingha Rap

Ya may think I'm good, ya may think I'm bad,
Ya may think I'm calm, ya may think I'm mad!
But hang on to your chairs, I'll blow your mind,
I'll think of something that won't leave you behind.
A bib, a bob, a bib bib bob!
I'm giving you all the Weerasingha rap!

I was born on the 3rd of June,
I thought I was going to come out soon.
I was in my mother squeezed up tight,
I could see my mother having a fright!
I wanted to laugh, I wanted to shout,
I was so happy, I pounced out!

I was so thrilled I wanted to leave!
Then I heard some people give a shout,
"One push, Mrs Priangica, and she'll be out."
I'm telling you that was a puzzle to me,
I shouted, "Hey! How did you know I'm a she?"
The midwife shouted, "Good lord, she can talk!"
I popped out my head and said, "You want a
speech?"

I talked and talked around that room,
Balam bam boolah, balam da diddy boom.
A bib, a bob, a bib bib bob,
I'm giving you all the Weerasingha rap!

When I was one, I crawled around the ground,
When I was two, I ate something that I found.
When I was three, I started to walk,
When I was four, I started to talk.
When I was five, I rode my bike,
When I was six, I caught my own pike!
When I was seven, I went to school,
When I was eight, I grew tall.
When I was nine, I came to England,
When I was ten, I met Mr Finlan!
So that's what I am, that's what I'll be,
With a C, with an H, with an A and gee.
So that's what I am, that's what I'll be,
Miss Chagee, Miss Wathma, Miss Sister, Miss Me!

Wathma Weerasingha (10)

Ferndale Primary School, Great Barr

This Is Me

You may think I'm short, you may think I'm poor,
You may think I'm dumb, you may think I'm a plum,
But hang on to your seats and listen right here,
I'm gonna tell you something that will blow your ears.
A tick, a tock, a tick-tock tack,
I'm giving you all the Samuel Bennett rap.

I was born on the 17th of May, hooray!
I remember very well that awful day.
I was in Mother, but I was curled up tight,
Though I have to say it was dark as midnight,
Like a forest at night,
I was in a tomb like a broom.
Then I hears some people give a shout!

I'm telling you, that was a puzzle to me,
I shouted out, "How do you know I'm a he?!"
Doctor shouted, "Oh lord he can talk!"
Then I said, "Now watch me walk."
I walked and talked again and again,

A tick, a tock, a tick-tock tack,
I'm giving you all the Samuel Bennet rap (rap, rap, rap).

When I was one, I ate my dog's poo,
When I was two, I missed the loo for a number two,
When I was three, I got thinner,
When I was four, I ate the dog's dinner,
When I was five, I saw a boar,
When I was six, I missed a ball,
When I was seven, I dreamt of heaven,
When I was eight, I made my first mate,
When I was nine, I was full of joy,
When I was ten, I jumped on a boy.

So that's what I am, that's what I'll be,
With an S, with an A, with an M, with a U, with an E
and with an L,
Mr Sam, Mr Samuel, Mr Bennett, Mr Me.
A tick, A tock, A tick-tock tack,
I'm giving you all the Samuel Bennett rap.
(Rap, rap, rap, rap, rap, rap, rap).

Samuel Bennett (10)

Ferndale Primary School, Great Barr

The Zahra Rahman Rap

You may think I'm bossy, you may think I'm mad,
You may think I'm crazy or may think I'm bad.
But hang on to your horses and listen right here,
Bip, bop, bip bip bop!
I'm giving you the Zahra's rap! (rap, rap, rap)

I was born on the 26th of May,
I remember that very great day.
I was in my mother, curled up tight,
My poor mother must have had a fright!
Living freely, no worries on my mind,
I was so happy, be left behind.

Then I heard some doctors give a shout,
"One more push Mrs Rahman, and she'll be out!"
I'm telling you that confused me,
I shouted out, "How do you know I'm a she?"
Doctor shouted, "Oh god she can talk!"
I peeked out my head and said, "Now watch me walk!"
I jumped and jived around the room,
Balam bam boolah, balam ba diddy boom.

I'm giving you all the Zahra Rahman (rap, rap, rap)

When I was one I crawled around the chairs,
When I was two I grew brown hairs.
When I was three I started walking,
When I was four I started talking.
When I was five I started school,
When I was six I got a pool.
When I was seven I got taller,
When I was eight I became a good drawer.
When I was nine I got my first pet,
When I was ten I wanted to be a vet.

So that's what I am, that's what I'll be,
With a Z, with an A, with an H, with an R, with an A.
So that's what I am, that's what I'll be,
Miss Zahra, Miss Sister, Miss Rahman, Miss Me.
A bip, a bop, a bip bip bop,
I'm giving you all the Zahra Rahman rap (rap, rap, rap)

Zahra Rahman (10)
Ferndale Primary School, Great Barr

This Is Me

You may think I'm cool, you may think I'm bad,
You may think I'm strong, you may think I'm bland.
But hang on to your seats and listen right there,
I'm gonna tell you something that will make you stare.
A hip, a hop, a hip hop hap,
I'd like to introduce you to the Alyaan Raja rap.

I was born on the 14th of July,
I remember the days when I used to cry.
When I was little I liked to watch TV,
I remember the days when life used to be easy.
I went to the doctors to check me out,
Then I said, "What is this all about?"
The doctor said, "How does he know how to speak?"
Then I replied, "I've been doing it for a week."
Now that I've got a sister,
It's as if she is the prime minister.
And now that I've got another one,
It seems as if the nightmare will never be gone.

A hip, a hop, a hip hop hap,
I'm giving you all the Alyaan Raja rap.

When I was one, I held a bat,
When I was two, I fell off a flat.
When I was three I broke an arm,
When I was four, I raided a farm.
When I was five, I scored a goal,
When I was six, I dug up a hole.
When I was seven, I rode a bike,
When I was eight I went on a hike.
When I was nine, I swam in a tank,
When I was ten, I robbed the bank.

So that's what I am, that's what I'll be,
With an A, with an L, with a Y.
So that's what I am, that's what I'll be,
Mr Aly, Mr Alyaan, Mr Raja, Mr Me.
A hip, a hop, a hip hop hap,
I'm giving you all the Alyaan Raja rap.

Alyaan Raja (10)

Ferndale Primary School, Great Barr

The Maiya Chattu Wrap

You may think I'm dumb, you may think I'm a plum,
You may think I'm mad, you may think I'm sad,
But hang on to your souls and listen right here,
I'm gonna tell ya something that will make you
disappear,
A hip, a hop, a hip hop hap,
I'm giving you all the Maiya Chattu rap.

I was born on the 19th of July,
I remember very well that awful day,
I was in my mother, curled up tight,
Though I have to say it was dark as midnight!
Nothing to do didn't wanna breathe,
I was so happy, didn't wanna leave,
Then I hear some people give a shout,
"One push and she'll be all out!"
I'm telling you, that was a puzzle to me,
I shouted, "How do you know I'm a she?"
The doctor shouted "Oh lord she can talk!"
I popped out my head and said, "Now watch me
walk!"

A hip a hop, a hip hop hap,
I'm giving you all the Maiya Chattu rap.

When I was 1, I bathed in the sink,
When I was 2, I started to blink,
When I was 3, I got hit by a bat,
When I was 4, I got scratched by a cat,
When I was 5, I got made a sister,
When I was 6, I became prime minister,
When I was 7, I got trapped in a machine,
When I was 8, I had an awful dream,
When I was 9, I closed all the schools,
When I was 10, I became queen of the fools.

With an M, with an A, with an I, with a Y, with an A,
So that's what I am, that's what I'll be,
Miss Maiya, Miss Chattu, Miss me,
A tic toc, tic toc tak,
I'm giving you all the Maiya Chattu rap.

Maiya Chattu (10)
Ferndale Primary School, Great Barr

This Is Me

Ya may think I'm sassy, ya may think I'm classy,
Ya may think I'm crazy, ya may think I'm lazy.
But hold your horses,
I'll open your minds,
Ensuring that none is left behind!
Beep bop, beep bop bap!
I'm giving you all the Isabel rap!

I was born on the 15th of July,
I came out pretty sly.
I was born a gymnast, coming out in a handstand,
Landing perfectly showing everyone a right hand.
I was so happy, showing my moves.

I heard some people giving a hurl!
"Congrats Mrs Blythe, it's a girl!"
That really confused me!
"How ya know I'm a girl!?"
Midwife said, "Good lord it can talk!"
"Now watch me dance!"

Ha, he, ha he hap,
Beep, bop, beep bop bap,
I'm giving you all the Isabel rap!

When I was one, I swam 800 metres,
When I was two, I drank some litres.
When I was three, I plucked some fleas,
When I was four, I hated peas.
When I was five, I climbed a beehive,
When I was six, I learned to give a high-five.
When I was seven, I stole a chicken,
When I was eight, I kept on lickin'.
When I was nine, I got a lizard,
When I was ten, I met a wizard.

So that's who I am, that's what I've done.

With an I, with an S,
With an A, with a B,
With an E, with an L.

So that's who I am and that's what I've done.
Miss Isabel, Miss Hunter,
Miss Sister, Miss Me!

Beep! bop, beep bop bap,
I'm giving you all the Isabel rap!

Isabel Hunter (10)
Ferndale Primary School, Great Barr

This Is Me

A kennings poem

A Roblox gamer
A stubborn blamer
A creative cooker
A focused looker
A sporty soul
An artistic drawer
An athletic runner
A high jumper
An epic swimmer
A brave walker
A messy eater
A poor cheater
This is me!
Jia!

Jia Chaudhry (10)
Ferndale Primary School, Great Barr

Anna Higgins Rap

Ya may think I'm smart, you may think I'm dumb,
Ya may think I'm fun, ya may think I'm dull.
But hang on to your seats and listen right there,
I'm gonna tell you something that'll make you
disappear!
A tick, a tock, a tick tock tap,
I'm giving you all the Anna Higgins rap!

I was born on the 29th of the 9th,
I visualize this very same night,
I was in my mother curled up tight.
Thought I had to admit, it was dark as midnight!
Very bored, nothing to do,
Maybe I remember my first poo!

When I hear a sudden shout,
One last push and I was out.
It was all a puzzle to me,
But how did they know I was a she!?
I shot out like a rocket going to space,
I came out with a very angry face!

A tick, a tock, a tick-tock tap,
I'm giving you all the Anna Higgins rap!

When I was one I talked to a knife,
When I was two my brother came to life!
When I was three I started getting thinner,
When I was four I ate the dog's dinner.
When I was five I kicked a ball,
When I was six I became quite tall.
When I was seven I dreamed I was eleven,
When I was eight I scored seven.
When I was nine I was on a football team,
When I was ten I watched all the teachers beam!

So that's what I am, so that's what I'll be.
With an A, with an N, with an N, with an A.
So that's what I am, so that's what I'll be,
Mrs Anna, Mrs Banana, Mrs Higgins, Mrs Me.
A tick, a tock, a tick-tock tap,
I'm giving you all the Anna Higgins rap.

Anna Higgins (11)

Ferndale Primary School, Great Barr

This Is Me Jasleen

You may think I'm bright, you may think I'm cool,
You may think I'm silly, you may think I'm a fool.
But hang on to your seats and listen right here,
I'm going to tell you something that will burn your ears.
A hip, a hop, a hip hop hap.
I'm giving you all the Jasleen Neer rap.

I was born on the 2nd of December,
That's a special day I will always remember.
I was in my mother's arms, curled up tight,
I opened my eyes and was blinded by a light.
I was so comfy you would not believe,
I didn't know what I would achieve.

A year later my brother was here,
His crying was all I could hear.
"Wa wa wa, chichi wa."
A hip, a hop, a hip hop hap,
I'm giving you all the Jasleen Neer rap.

When I was one I became a big sister,
When I was two I became the prime minister.
When I was three I picked up a feather,
When I was four I checked the weather.
When I was five I danced the tango,
When I was six I ate a mango.
When I was seven I became quite tall,
When I was eight I played dodgeball.
When I was nine I fell in love with cake,
When I was ten I learned how to bake.
And that's what I am, that's what I'll be,
With a J, with an A, with an S, with an L, with an E,
with an E, with an N.

So that's what I am and that's what I'll be,
Mrs Jasleen, Mrs Jas, Mrs Neer, Mrs Me.
A hip, a hop, a hip hop hap,
I'm giving you all the Jasleen Neer rap.

Jasleen Neer (10)

Ferndale Primary School, Great Barr

This Is Me

You may think I'm joyful, you may think I'm dull,
You may think I'm bad, you may think I'm fun,
But hang on to your seats and listen right here,
I'm going to tell you something that will burst you
into laughing tears.
A tip tap tippity tip tap,
I'm giving you all the Noah Saur rap.

I was born on the sixth of May,
Inside my mother, Theresa May,
I remember that terrible day,
Waking up in a bay, sadly no one said, "Hooray!"
So I slipped out and said, "Hey!"
The doctor stepped up and said, "Oh golly gosh, he
can talk!"
So I went up to him and said, "Oi! You big stork."
So I went up to walk and started singing,
Bam boom, bim bop pow,
A tip tap tippity tap,
I'm giving you all the Noah Saur rap.

When I was one I went to the moon,
When I was two I jumped in goo.
When I was three I climbed a tree,
When I was four I rode a boar.
When I was five I said, "I'm alive."
When I was six, I ate my nan's biscuits.
When I was seven, I went to Devon.
When I was eight, I got a pet ape.
When I was nine, I closed all the schools,
When I was ten they made me king of the cools!
So that's what I am, that's what I'll be.

With an N, with an O,
With an A, with an H.
So that's what I am, that's what I'll be,
Mr Noah, Mr Finley, Mr Sargent, Mr Me.
A tip tap tippity tip tap,
I'm giving you all the Noah Saur rap.

Noah Sargent (10)
Ferndale Primary School, Great Barr

This Is Me

You may think I'm bright,
You may think I'm a spark.
You may think I'm a queen,
You may think I'm dark.
But hang on to your seats,
And listen right here.
I'm gonna tell you something that will shrivel up
your hair.
A hip, a hop, a hip hop hap,
I'm giving you all the Keanna Rose rap.
(Rap, rap, rap)

I was born on the 26th of December,
A very special day that I will remember.
I was a present wrapped up tight,
I shone bright like a Christmas light.
Though I have to say,
It was dark as midnight,
Nothing to do, nothing to see.
I was so shy you wouldn't believe!
A hop, a hop, a hip hop hap,
I'm giving you all the Keanna Rose rap!

When I was one, I danced the macarena!
When I was two, I couldn't hear ya!
When I was three, I got a rabbit!
When I was four, I gave it a carrot!
When I was five, I had a baby brother!
When I was six, I met the Queen's mother!
When I was seven, I became a sister!
When I was eight, I became the prime minister!
When I was nine, I became a dancer!
When I was ten, I became the world's biggest prancer!

So that's what I am, that's what I'll be, with a K-e-a-n-n-a,
So that's what I am, that's what I'll be, Miss Daniels, Miss Keanna, Miss Me.
A hip, hop, a hip hop hap,
I'm giving you all the Keanna Rose Daniels rap.
(Rap, rap, rap).

Keanna Daniels (10)

Ferndale Primary School, Great Barr

This Is Me

You may think I'm bright, you may think I'm dull,
You may think I'm empty, you may think I'm full.
But hold on to your seats and listen right there,
I'm gonna tell you something that will blow your hair.
A hip, a hop, a hip hop hap,
I'm giving you all the NT rap.

I was born on the 29th of May,
I remember very well that joyous day,
I was curled in my mom really tight,
She was really kind of fat, I'm not gonna lie.
Nothing to do, nothing to play,
I kind of remember my moms' gruesome face.
A hip, a hop, a hip hop hap,
I'm giving you all the NT rap.

When I was one I set off a bomb,
When I was two I heard a cow moo.
When I was three I did my first pee,
When I was four I cut my knee.

When I was five I went for a dive,
When I was six I learnt how to drive.
When I was seven I dreamt of heaven,
When I was eight I made a mate.
When I was nine I climbed the vine,
When I was ten I kicked a hen.

So that's who I am and that's who I'll be.
With an N, with an E, with an H-A-N,
So that's who I am and that's who I'll be.
Mr Nae, Mr Nehan, Mr Tanvir, Mr Me.
A hip, a hop, a hip hop hap,
I'm giving you all the NT rap.

Nehan Tanvir (10)
Ferndale Primary School, Great Barr

Tay Tay Rap

Ya may think I'm dying
Ya may think I'm sighing
But if you are my foe
So I'm gonna let you know
That this awesome beat
May turn up the heat
No cap
But listen to the Tay Tay rap

I was born in March on the 28th
And boy my mom had a lot of faith
When I came out I had a big head
Then the doctor said
"Congratulations!"
That showed a lot of appreciation
No cap
So listen to the Tay Tay rap

When I was one I was fed some milk
When I was two I saw some silk
When I was three I ate an ice lolly
When I was four I heard someone say "Golly!"

When I was five I started to drool
When I was six I went to school
When I was seven I was in trouble
When I was eight I blew a bubble
When I was nine I ate a Cheeto
When I was ten I sang Despacito

No cap
So listen to the Tay Tay rap

After that, I grew so tall
Then I knew how to play ball
Once upon a time, I scored a hat-trick
Then I came up with an epic tactic
So all of this is about me
So maybe sit down and have a cup of tea
So that's what I am, and that's what I'll be
With a T, with an A, with a Y with and O
No cap
So listen to the Tay Tay rap.

Tayhon Elson (10)
Ferndale Primary School, Great Barr

Me, Me, Me!

Ya may think I'm funny, you may think I'm mad,
Ya may think I'm crazy, you may think I'm rad.
But hang on to your dogs because they're gonna fetch it!
And when they do you're gonna regret it!
A woof, a bark, a woof woof bark!
I'm giving you all the Esha Allport rap rap rap.

I was born on the 4th of June,
I thought I was coming out soon.
I was in my mom bunched up tight,
I probably gave her a big fat fright.

Then I heard some people give a shout,
"One big push Mrs Allport, then she'll be out."
I'm telling you that gave me a puzzle,
I shouted out, "How do you know I'm a she?"
Doctor shouted out, "Good lord she can talk!"
I popped out my head, "Now watch me walk!"

When I was one, I crawled around the chairs,
When I was two, I stole all my mom's pears.
When I was three, I fell into a lake,

When I was four, I choked on a cornflake.
When I was five I sat on my nan's dogs,
When I was six I fell on some logs.

When I was seven, I joined a football team,
When I was eight, I became the queen.
When I was nine, I cut my fringe,
When I was ten, I had a sweety binge!

Esha Allport (10)
Ferndale Primary School, Great Barr

The Peter Wright Rap

You may think I'm bright, you may think I'm dull,
You may think I'm fun, you may think I'm dumb.

But hang on to your seats and listen closely,
I'm going to tell you something that will make you stare.
A hip hop, a hip hop hap,
I'm going to tell all the Peter Wright rap.

I remember that very day in Mother during the night,
But I have to say it was the darkest night I have ever seen.
Some people were shouting out, "Push Misses Wright."
She pushed me out and I said, "Oh it's you again."
The doctor said, "God he can talk!"
A hip, hop, hip hop hap,
I'm giving you the Peter Wright rap.

When I was 1, I ate a bag of plums.
When I was 2, I had two thumbs.
When I was 3, I fell out of a tree.

When I was 4, I did a chore.
When I was 5, I had a PS5.
When I was 6, I hit a wall with a brick.
When I was 7, I went to heaven.
When I was 8, I opened a gate.
When I was 9, I had a hard time.
When I was 10, I drop-kicked a hen.

So that's what I am and that's what I'll be,
Mr Peter, Mr Rabbit, Mr Me.

Peter Wright (10)

Ferndale Primary School, Great Barr

The Big AK

Ya may think I'm slower
You may think I'm faster
If you think none listen to this rapper
I'm gonna burn your ear
I hope you heard that clear
But now you know Arjan is here
Right now you know you're listening to the king rapper
At Christmas I always pull a cracker
I support West Brom that's the best
Nasty Villa are such a pest
I hate Wolves as well, they're so bad
When they score I go so mad.

I was born on the 9th March
I remember that day, I did a trick on a go-kart
I was only one, it was the very very start
I was in the army, they told me to march
I was so rich I had the bucks
When I was small I had the looks

When I was one I won the cup final
When I was two I met Lionel
When I was three I scored a hat-trick
When I was four I came up with a new tactic
When I was five I was hitting straight As
When I was six Wolves were bottom, yeah, hooray
When I was seven Baggies were top
When I was eight I was caught by the cops
When I was nine I was in year five
When I was ten I did a dive.

Arjan Klaar (10)

Ferndale Primary School, Great Barr

This Is Me

You may think I'm kind, you may think I'm harsh,
You may think I'm happy, you may think I'm sad,
But hang on to your seats and listen,
Right here I'm gonna tell you something that's
gonna blow your ears,
Hip hop hip hop, I'm giving you all the Juvrajan
Barnes rap.
I was born on the 24th of September,
I remember very well, it was an awful day,
I was in my mom curled up tight,
There was nothing to do, didn't wanna leave,
The doctor said, "God gracious, he can talk!"
I responded, "How did you know I was a he?"

When I was one I went to Antarctica,
When I was two I ate a bag of fruits,
When I was three I fell off a tree,
When I was four I watched The Fantastic Four,
When I was five I went for a drive,
When I was six I became the 6th prime minister,
When I was seven I counted up to 11,
When I was eight, I ate the cat's dinner,

When I was nine I drank a glass of wine,
When I was ten I visited Big Ben,
That's who I am and that's who I'll be,
J-u-v-y.

Juvrajan Barnes (11)
Ferndale Primary School, Great Barr

The I Rap

Ya may think I'm happy, ya may think I'm sad
Ya may think I'm happy, ya may think I'm mad
Hold on to your horses and get ready for the beat
Go to the cinema, book a place for your seat
A hip, hop, hip hip hap
I'm giving you all the big Rassool rap

I was born with my dad eating chicken
It was so good it was finger lickin'
My sister was holding on very tight
Until she came out late one night
My grandparents were my company as well
My dad was asleep as if under a spell
What do you think of my story so far
I know what you think, I am a twinkling star

When I was one I had a long nap
When I was two I ate good porridge
When I was three I could say hi
When I was four I played for West Bromwich
When I was five I gave a high five

When I was six I went to school
When I was seven I got my pen license
When I was eight my teacher said "You are cool!"
When I was nine I could sing
When I was ten they said Joe Biden will win.

Ibrahim Rassool (10)

Ferndale Primary School, Great Barr

The Mali Z Rap

My name is Maliha and I'm ecstatic to say
Ya may think I'm happy, ya may think I'm mad
I could be zeal, I could be bad
And yes I'm about to sing a rap
So hold your hips
And lend some tips
You're listening to the Maliha Zia rap
Mmm I would like a wrap

Tip tap tippity tap
I was born on 27th of September
I love cucumber
I remember being caved in
When I was in my mother
I hoped to not have a brother
I remember being tight at night
Getting ready to fight
One more squeeze and out I popped
Holding on, out I dropped
Snip, snap, snippet snap

When I was one I was a dime
When I was two I made a serious crime
When I was three I robbed a bank
When I was four I swam in a pool and sank
When I was five I karate chopped a door
When I was six I was poor
When I was seven I became the earth
When I was eight I gave birth
When I was nine I was a bug
When I was ten my laptop's memory was dug.

Maliha Zia (11)
Ferndale Primary School, Great Barr

The Megster Rap

My name is Megan and I'm happy to say
You may think I'm crazy, you may think I'm mad
I could be cheerful, I could be sad
So hold your hats
I'll be glad
I do have a dog
I don't have a cat
But who knows, let's get on with the rap

Tip tap tippity tap
So let's begin
I was born 27th September
My sis was born in November
I remember, snug and tight
Until I saw a little light
One more squeeze and out I popped
Still holding on
She's a girl, she's a girl
Ow I screamed
I was in a good dream
Tip tap tippity tap

When I was one I caught the flu
When I was two I lived in a zoo
When I was three I went shopping at the mall
When I was four I went running in a pool
When I was five I ran a school
When I was six I looked too cool
When I was seven I became a mathematician
When I was eight I was into fashion
When I was nine I at the Milky Way
When I was ten my dog flew away.

Megan Pickford (11)
Ferndale Primary School, Great Barr

The Ella Ashby Rap

Ya may think I'm happy
Ya may think I'm sad
Ya may think I'm crazy
Ya may think I'm mad
But hold your horses and listen right here
I'm gonna tell ya something that will burn your
ears

I was born on the 14th of September 2010
I'm eleven years old and I remember the day when
I was born in West Brom as I'm the bomb
So I'm going to tell you all about the day
I was born the day my nan and grandad went
away
I was two weeks late
So I had to come away
A hip hop, a hip hop hap
I'm telling you all the Ella Ashby rap

When I was one I made a movie
When I was two I danced really groovy

When I was three I brought a dog
When I was four I jumped over the bog
When I was five I got a fiver
When I was six I became a miner
When I was seven I robbed a bank
When I was eight I met someone called Frank
When I was nine I closed all the pools
When I was ten I became queen of the fools.

Ella Ashby (11)
Ferndale Primary School, Great Barr

Ethan's Rap

Ya may think I'm cryin'
Ya may think I'm dyin'
Ya may think I'm a lion
Ya may think I'm flyin'
But hold onto your hats
And sit back down
Cos I'm about to drop a beat
That is gonna be lit

A music maker
A motivator
A ball kicker
A messy gamer
A team player
An electric energiser
A potato hater
A game maker

My name is Ethan, I love to play football
I've been playing since I was small

My mom once said "You were always kicking in my belly
The only thing that could make you stop was a bowl of jelly."

When I was one I started to talk
When I was two I started to walk
When I was three I cut a tree
When I was four I broke a door
When I was five I wanted more
When I was six I made a cake
When I was seven I started to bake
When I was eight I ran across a pitch
When I was nine I fell in a ditch
When I was ten I did it all again.

Ethan Dodge-Pace (10)
Ferndale Primary School, Great Barr

Eniola's Rap

Ya may think I'm weak
Ya ma think I'm meek
But listen to me
And dance to the beat
I might be happy
I might be sad
So go on, and tell your dad
This is me
And who I wanna be
I can't change that for
You, he and she

Hip hop hippity hop
You may think I'm lazy
But I'm actually crazy
I was born in a hospital
Like how is it possible
All the attention was
All. On. Me.
Until I was three
It fell into a breeze

When I was one I started to talk
When I was two I started to walk
When I was three I ate my dog's dinner
When I was four I got a lot thinner
When I was five I became a snitcher
When I was six I became richer
When I was seven my cousin turned eleven
When I was eight someone went to heaven
When I was nine I grew tall
When I was ten I opened a door.

Eniola Adeyemi (10)
Ferndale Primary School, Great Barr

I Am Arun, This Is Me

Ya may think I'm slow
Ya may think I'm fast
Ya may think I'm bad but I'm really sad
When you hear a boom you know I was due on the
29th of June
On that day my mom was doomed with a big bam
boom
My name is Arun and I like playing dodgeball
I've always enjoyed it ever since I was small

When I was one I liked eating ham
When I was two I sat next to a fan
When I was three I found my dad's keys
When I was four I counted to three
When I was five I went to school
When I was six I jumped in a pool
When I was seven I became the king of rap
When I was eight I looked at a map
When I was nine I ate a cake
When I was ten I copied Drake

Geography hater
Fortnite gamer
Maths lover
Ferndale fighter
Faithful friend
Mindful memories
Bad listener

This is me!

Arun Dhadley
Ferndale Primary School, Great Barr

Calum Balum Rap

Ya may think I'm happy
Ya may think I'm sad
Ya may think I'm crazy
Ya may think I'm bad
You better sit on a chair
And this might burn your ears
Because I'm giving you one sick beat
A hip hop a hip hop hap
I'm giving you the Calum Balum rap

When I was one, I was a star
When I was two, I went to a bar
When I was three, I got a lot bigger
When I was four, I learned to drive a digger
When I was five I had a beer
When I was six I ate a deer
No cap, listen to the Calum Balum rap
When I was seven I met Venom
When I was eight I ate a lemon
When I was nine I got a dog
When I was ten I named him Bog
No cap, listen to the Calum Balum rap

With a C, with an A, with an L
Mr Cal, Mr Calum
Mr Robinson, Mr Me
No cap, listen to the Calum Balum rap.

Calum Robinson-Ash (10)

Ferndale Primary School, Great Barr

The Mad TT Rap

You may think I'm mad
You may think I'm crazy
You may even think I stomp on a daisy
But hold your horses you can sit right there
I'm looking like the Fresh Prince of Belair
When I was born I was looking so fly
When people looked they would die

I like to eat
I like to sleep
Now watch me as I drop this sick beat
I love my fashion
And singing is my passion
A boom a bam a boom and a bam
I'm giving you all the TT rap.

When I was one I hugged a snake
When I was two I loved to bake
At three I rode a bike
At four I sang into a mic
When I was five I played in slime
When I was six, I ate a lime

At seven, I played in a band
At eight, I ate sand
When I was nine I had a lovely picnic
When I was ten I put on red lipstick.

Tia Williams (10)

Ferndale Primary School, Great Barr

The Baddie GZ Rap

You may think I'm bad
You may think I'm mad
But hold your horses and listen to my rap
When I was born I was looking so swag
That even the doctors fell on their back

I like to eat
I like to sleep
I also like listening to some beats
I make my own fashion
And I have a good passion

When I was one I fell in a puddle
When I was two I liked to cuddle
When I was three I liked to bake
When I was four I ate a cake
When I was five I licked a mic
When I was six I rode a bike
When I was seven I sang a song
When I was eight I played along

When I was nine I made a rhyme
When I was ten I played a mime

This is me!

Giulia Zainea (10)
Ferndale Primary School, Great Barr

This Is MW

A kennings poem

A fantastic footballer
A tremendous person
A motivated person
An intelligent person
An epic gamer
An athletic person
A sporty person
A smart person
A scuba diver
A Manchester supporter
A wise person
A lot of experience
An active person
A Ronaldo fan
A traveller
A caring person
A kind person
A hard-working person
A leader
An artistic person

A creative person
A funny person
A swimmer
A confident person
A respectful person
A photographer
A good teamworker
This is Mikolaj.

Mikolaj Wardawa (10)
Ferndale Primary School, Great Barr

I Am A

A kennings poem

Pro gamer,
Great achiever,
Cat lover,
Brilliant learner,
Strong believer,
Eager approver,
Badminton player,
An open thinker,
Nervous speaker,
Play maker.
Put this together,
I'm Lucas.

Lucas Smith (10)
Ferndale Primary School, Great Barr

Me, Me, Me

A kennings poem

A kind person,
A great achiever,
A joyful dancer,
A fearless creator,
An excellent egg maker,
A success planner,
A determined chatter,
A resilient persuader,
A funny partner.
I am Tayvia.

Tayvia Hylton (10)
Ferndale Primary School, Great Barr

This Is Me

A kennings poem

A excellent hard worker,
A fantastic footballer,
A evolutionary gamer,
A immature troublemaker,
A mature Muslim,
A chatty chatterbox,
A loyal companion,
Put these together,
I'm Mustafa.

Mustafa Rehman (10)

Ferndale Primary School, Great Barr

True Colours

Some flowers are red,
Some flowers are blue,
You might not see it but...
You're beautiful as you.

They will try and try
To get your spirits down,
But do not cry
You deserve the crown!

Mazy Smith (11)
Ferndale Primary School, Great Barr

This Is Me

A kennings poem

A motivated person,
An outstanding friend,
A minor child,
An independent human,
A fantastic sister,
A hard worker,
A loyal friend,
Put this all together...
I'm Isabelle.

Isabelle Harrington

Ferndale Primary School, Great Barr

This Is Me

A kennings poem

Super smart,
A clumsy climber,
An ambitious achiever,
An eager learner,
An exceptional artist,
An elegant student,
A hard worker.

Put them together and you get James.

James Mills (10)
Ferndale Primary School, Great Barr

This Is Me

A kennings poem

A hard worker,
A kind friend,
A world-recorder,
An amazing dancer,
A good singer,
A handwriting champion,
A loving person.
Put these together, I'm...
Miruna!

Miruna Luca

Ferndale Primary School, Great Barr

All About JJ

A kennings poem

Football lover
Neymar fan
Music listener
YouTube watcher
Roblox player
Prank master
Food gobbler
Positive person
Big achiever
This is what makes me Jarred.

Jarred Jonas (10)
Ferndale Primary School, Great Barr

This Is Me

A kennings poem

An active adventurer!
A quick learner!
A clumsy climber!
A confident carer!
A big brother!
A chatty child!
A motivating Muslim!
Put these together, I'm Umar!

Umar Faruki (10)
Ferndale Primary School, Great Barr

This Is Me Ashton

A kennings poem

A kind person,
A successful singer,
A peaceful human,
A cool fixer,
A powerful writer,
A mindful learner,
A big brother,
Put these together and you get Ashton.

Ashton Carr (10)

Ferndale Primary School, Great Barr

This Is Me Poppy

A kennings poem

A nice person,
A successful swimmer,
A chatty person,
A warm heart,
A quick learner,
An only child,
A dog person,
Put that all together and you get Poppy.

Poppy Rollins (10)
Ferndale Primary School, Great Barr

I Am Me!

A kennings poem

I am a mindful player,
More quieter,
An English winner,
Quick finisher,
Epic runner,
Active helper,
Cat lover.
Put these together,
I am Sahar Khan.

Sahar Khan (11)
Ferndale Primary School, Great Barr

This Is Me

A kennings poem

A healthy eater,
A cheeky chatterer,
A food muncher,
An epic runner,
A problem solver,
A dog lover,
A cat hater.
Put this together I am...
Tiana.

Tiana Lugha (10)
Ferndale Primary School, Great Barr

This Is Me

A kennings poem

A British Jamaican,
An amazing baller,
An ambitious sportsman,
An anime watcher,
A bubblegum dealer,
A money maker,
A loyal brother,
I am... Luke.

Luke-Curdie Powell (10)
Ferndale Primary School, Great Barr

Guess Who I Am

A kennings poem

I am...
A brilliant footballer,
A dog lover,
A vast achiever,
A whistle-blower,
A pro gamer,
A comical joker,
A clumsy faller.
I am N-I-K-O.

Niko Paszowski (10)
Ferndale Primary School, Great Barr

All About Me

A kennings poem

A dog lover,
A game lover,
A slow eater,
A fast runner,
A great listener,
A kind helper,
A great reader,
A football player.
I am Adam

Adam Gardner (10)

Ferndale Primary School, Great Barr

This Is Me

A kennings poem

Loving daughter
Twin sister
Motivated learner
Hard worker
Loyal friend
Trustworthy
Dream chaser
Put this together, I'm...
Elena.

Elena Smith (10)
Ferndale Primary School, Great Barr

This Is Me

A kennings poem

A confident questioner,
A quick runner,
An epic defender,
A good helper,
A funny joker,
A resilient learner,
A kind brother.
I am Ollie.

Ollie Bolton (10)

Ferndale Primary School, Great Barr

This Is Me

A kennings poem

A cheerful annoyance,
A creative being,
An admired act,
A peaceful pride,
A rare dreamer,
An honest spirit,
Scarlett.

Scarlett Aitchison (10)
Ferndale Primary School, Great Barr

I Am

A kennings poem

I am a super skater,
I am a strawberry lover.
I am a family lover.
I am a milkshake lover.
I am a great skater.
I am a French lover,
I am an art lover.
My eyes are blue.
My hair is gold.
I am a great helper,
I am a hard worker.
I am a TV lover.
I am a fast sleeper,
I am a fly wacker,
I am a fidget lover,
I am a sweet lover,
I am a dog lover,
I am an ice cream lover.

Lauren Mitchell (7)
Laira Green Primary School, Laira

This Is Me

A kennings poem

I am a jigsaw lover,
I am a flower lover,
I am a book lover.
I am a tree lover,
I am a sewer lover,
I am a fidget lover.
I am a colourer lover,
I am a puppy lover,
I am a school lover.
I am an ice cream lover,
I am a making lover,
I am a tree lover.
I am a baker lover,
I am a unicorn lover,
I am a good helper.
I am a listener,
I am a fidget lover,
This is me.

Layla-May Redgrave (7)

Laira Green Primary School, Laira

This Is Me

T he family of my town are the best,
H ulk is my favourite Avenger
I saiah is my brother and he's the best,
S pider-Man is my friends' favourite Avenger.

I saiah and me hang out with the gang,
S ponge cakes are delicious.

M y friend Leo is the coolest,
E melia is my girlfriend and she's the one.

Elijah Romeo (8)
Laira Green Primary School, Laira

Isaiah Is Me

I love the seaside,
S eeing friends and my girlfriend makes me happy,
A n excellent drawer,
I love eating jam,
A fan of Mr Beast and other YouTubers,
H ungry for adventure.

I saiah is my name,
S taying healthy.

M y brother is Elijah,
E lijah is my brother for life.

Isaiah Romeo (8)
Laira Green Primary School, Laira

Me

A kennings poem

I am a...
Quiet talker,
School lover,
Smart learner,
Dog walker,
Big sister,
Books reader,
Horror movie watcher,
Caring helper,
Sports lover,
Rugby player,
Kind daughter,
Fast runner,
Nature lover,
Craft maker,
Poem writer,
And finally a...
Wolf lover!

Amie Grimwood (9)
Laira Green Primary School, Laira

Me

A kennings poem

I am a Happy Meal eater,
I am a hamster lover,
I am a scooter rider,
I am a trampoline jumper,
I am a snack eater,
I am a dog lover,
I am a swimmer,
I am a TV watcher,
I am a Fortnite player,
I am a beach lover,
I am a chocolate eater,
I am a football player,
That's me.

Maddison Mouele (7)

Laira Green Primary School, Laira

Me

A kennings poem

I am an amazing skater,
I am a good breakfast maker,
I am a good book reader,
I am a chocolate lover,
I am a deep sleeper,
I am a trick-or-treater,
I am a comic book reader,
I am an amazing swimmer,
I am a good helper,
I am a turtle owner,
And finally...
A good maths learner.

Kayden Jones (8)
Laira Green Primary School, Laira

Free Poem

I am a snail tailor,
I am a video gamer.
I am a Ted for my sister,
I am a professional snail chef.
I digest dog food,
My eyes are brown.
My hair is wild,
My skin is white.
My age is 8,
I am a snail teaser,
I am a ghostbuster,
I am an amazing gymnast,
This is me.

Kacey Middleton (8)
Laira Green Primary School, Laira

I Am

I am a toy gun collector, ohh look at that one Dad!
I am a dog lover, woof, woof!
I am a van lover, argh the van didn't start again!
I am a coffee hater, yuck!
I am a cake lover, yum, yum!
I am a tea lover, yum!
I am a good helper,
My eyes are like the ocean,
This is me!

Noah Black (8)
Laira Green Primary School, Laira

Katie Lutley

A kennings poem

I am a...
Meat and chip lover,
McDonald's muncher,
Moon/Neonlight lover,
Dark forest addicted,
Crater lake (book) lover,
Guinea pig keeper,
Dog keeper/lover,
Sleeping lover,
Poop eyed,
Weird,
Fun lover,
Chatty,
And finally,
Caring person.

Katie Lutley (8)

Laira Green Primary School, Laira

I Am A

A kennings poem

I am a Twix eater,
I am a Mars eater,
I am an awesome boy,
My eyes are chocolate buttons,
My hair is conker-brown hair,
This is me.
Fast walker,
I am a book reader,
I am a loved boy,
I am a jumpy boy,
I am a long walker,
I am a good helper.

Freddie Baker-Truelove (7)

Laira Green Primary School, Laira

This Is Me

A kennings poem

I am a...
Minecraft lover,
Lego builder,
Horse lover,
TV lover,
Cuddle lover,
Bed lover,
Winter lover,
Drawing lover,
Food lover,
Cat lover,
Animal lover,
Chocolate lover,
Good listener,
Nature lover,
This is me.

Indigo Baker (8)

Laira Green Primary School, Laira

This Is Me

A kennings poem

I am...
Great gamer,
Chicken chaser,
Chicken player,
Book devourer,
Animal lover,
Front room polisher,
Game player,
Bathroom cleaner,
Art lover,
Guinea pig owner,
Guinea pig player,
And finally
Washing helper.

Violet Nicholls (8)
Laira Green Primary School, Laira

This Is Me

A kennings poem

I am a...
Bookworm,
Animal lover,
Friend maker,
Girl gamer,
Tiny cooker,
Expert crafter,
Loving sister,
Eco girl,
School councillor,
Rainbow lover,
Litter picker,
Good helper,
And finally...
Sweet girl.

Eloise Peart (8)

Laira Green Primary School, Laira

This Is Me

A kennings poem

I am a...
Professional eater,
Phone listener,
Awesome house janitor,
Baby player,
Messy snack gobbler,
Amazing hamster cleaner,
Curious detector,
Lonely passenger,
And finally...
An animal lover.

Shianna Dawson (9)
Laira Green Primary School, Laira

Leo

L iterally a big Marvel, Sonic and Godzilla fan.

E ating-machine when it comes to noodles, hot dogs and sausage rolls.

O ctopus are great and so is Lego, and my family is the best thing ever and so are my friends.

Leo Parker (9)

Laira Green Primary School, Laira

I Am

A kennings poem

I am a Lego and Minecraft builder,
I am a Roblox player and pro-gamer,
I am a football player and book reader,
I am a car and bus liker,
I am a food lover, vegetable hater,
I am a computer lover, Avenger hater.

Ishan Dahal (7)

Laira Green Primary School, Laira

Emelia

E melia is my name,
M y favourite food is chocolate,
E lowen is my sister,
L ove all my family,
I love to sing and dance,
A ll my friends are great.

Emelia Turner (8)
Laira Green Primary School, Laira

This Is Me

T rick or treating,
H alloween,
I t is me,
S weets.

I s this me,
S chool is so much fun.

M e is perfect,
E asy.

Evie Wilde (8)
Laira Green Primary School, Laira

Kennings

A kennings poem

I am...
An amazing TV watcher,
A dog lover,
A cool artist,
A happy chef,
A wonderful gamer of Roblox,
A cool dog walker,
A lover of phones.

Honey Bolter (8)

Laira Green Primary School, Laira

This Is Me And The Only One There Is

A kennings poem

What am I?
I'm a,
Gaming master,
Cat cuddler,
Juice drinker,
Invention maker,
Car lover,
And finally,
A poem maker.

Freddie Jones (7)
Luira Green Primary School, Laira

I Am A...

A kennings poem

I am a...
Deep sleeper,
A spider killer,
YouTuber gamer,
Good helper,
Food robber,
Den maker,
Handwriter,
And finish.

Riley
Laira Green Primary School, Laira

I Am...

A kennings poem

Chocolate lover,
Football player,
Lego lover,
Easter lover,
Bick lover,
And finally,
A fidget lover.
This is me.

Emily Bogusiewicz (8)
Laira Green Primary School, Laira

Me

A kennings poem

I am a...
Dark chocolate lover,
A vegetable eater,
A good helper,
And finally...
A ginger daughter.

Amelie Collins (7)

Laira Green Primary School, Laira

I Am

A kennings poem

I am a...
Spider killer,
Chocolate eater,
Teddy hugger,
Sweet lover,
Dog walker.

Leo Cordy (7)
Laira Green Primary School, Laira

Rogue

A kennings poem

I am a
Bunny lover,
Cat helper,
Chocolate eater,
Bearded dragon feeder.

Rogue (7)

Laira Green Primary School, Laira

This Is Me

A great footballer,
L oves Manchester United,
E xcellent at maths,
X ylophone fan.

H appiest when playing football,
A mazing at defending,
R eally makes people laugh,
K nows how the Titanic sank,
N ever plays basketball,
E ager to learn new things,
S uper fast when running,
S nakes are amazing.

Alex Harkness (7)
McKinney Primary School, Dundrod

This Is Me

J olly jellyfish,
E xcellent at maths,
S purs fan,
S wimming lover,
E ngland fan.

W erner is super,
R eally thoughtful and kind,
I 'm a football fan,
G iraffes are one of my favourites!
H olland is a brilliant player,
T anks are very cool!

Jesse Wright (7)
McKinney Primary School, Dundrod

This Is Me

M onkeys are my favourite animals.
A crobatic.
C aring.
E lephants are my favourite zoo animal.
Y oghurts are delicious.

W histling all the time,
I am good at art,
L oves all animals,
S uper at maths,
O bedient and sensible,
N ever gives up.

Macey Wilson (7)

McKinney Primary School, Dundrod

This Is Me

W onderful Willow,

I gloo ice heart,

L iker of hamsters,

L ightning when running,

O bedient fish,

W hale lover.

I ce heart,

R ugby gem,

V ery good drawer,

I n the sea, I'm a fish,

N efertiti fan,

E nglish fan.

Willow Irvine (7)

McKinney Primary School, Dundrod

This Is Me

E xcellent at English,
L ovely little lion,
I ncredible with animals,
Z oologist in the future,
A mazing at hockey.

B rilliant baby bear,
E xquisite at dancing,
L ovely lobster,
L ovely lamb.

Eliza Bell (7)
McKinney Primary School, Dundrod

This Is Me

M ovie lover,

I ntelligent,

R eally kind,

I nquisitive mind,

A mazing at maths,

M aths whizz.

B rilliant baby bear,

E xcellent and kind,

L oves doing maths,

L ovely lobster.

Miriam Bell (7)

McKinney Primary School, Dundrod

This Is Me

C heerful cat,

H appy hedgehog,

L oving leopard,

O bedient octopus,

E xcellent elephant.

K icking kangaroo,

Y oung yak,

L earning lemur,

E xcited eel.

Chloe Kyle (8)

McKinney Primary School, Dundrod

All About Me

I am so fast at football like Ronaldo,
My favourite goalkeeper is Ederson.
I am as cheerful as a rabbit munching on honey
carrots.
I am a good snake keeper,
She is called Dora.
I am as fast as the speed of light on my quad.

William Stewart (8)
McKinney Primary School, Dundrod

This Is Me

M ovies are my favourite,
E lephants are my best animal,
A thletics is my favourite subject,
D olphins are my favourite sea animal,
O bedient and sensible,
W inning all the time.

Meadow O'Grady-Waite (7)
McKinney Primary School, Dundrod

Eli

E xcellent person,

L oves maths,

I have a BFF called Isaac.

K ind,

I n Oundle Road is where I live,

N ational website lover,

G reen killer movie fan.

Eli King (8)

McKinney Primary School, Dundrod

This Is Me

R eally good at maths,

E xcellent at video games,

U seful,

B etter at football than my brother,

E xcellent at parkour,

N ever gives up.

Reuben McKinstry (7)

McKinney Primary School, Dundrod

Jonathan

J umping jack,

O range lover,

N oisy,

A dventurous,

T errific at football,

H appy,

A crobatic,

N ever gives up.

Jonathan Simpson (8)

McKinney Primary School, Dundrod

Alfie

A m a mastermind at maths.
L ikes playing games.
F orever learning new facts about everything.
I love playing sports.
E njoys tacos and sushi.

Alfie Moses (8)
McKinney Primary School, Dundrod

This Is Me

I'm a killer koala,
I'm a Harry Potter fan!
I'm as cuddly as a sloth,
I'm stronger than an elephant,
I'm a monster muncher,
I'm a Netflix fan.

Jack Carson (7)
McKinney Primary School, Dundrod

This Is Me

I have a BFF called Eli

S nakes can kill you.

A Pop It is so fun,

A meme is so funny.

C an Mr Beast buy a Lamborghini?

Isaac Barber (7)
McKinney Primary School, Dundrod

Layla

L oves swimming,

A tall giraffe,

Y oung cyclist,

L iving calculator,

A cat lover.

Layla Carlisle (8)
McKinney Primary School, Dundrod

All About Me

I am a nature lover.
I am a good friend.
I am a super conker hunter.
I am fun.
This is me.

Jenson Minford (7)
McKinney Primary School, Dundrod

Arobi

H i! I'm Arobi,
I 'm...

A book worm,
R ude when you're not nice,
O ptimistic and unique,
B eautiful and...
I ntelligent.

My hobbies are to...

R ead and write,
E at lots of food,
A nd I also like drawing,
L ove my family and I'm sometimes...
L onely,
Y ou'd really want to be my friend.

And...

I f I were you, Arobi would never be lonely because,

S he would already be my friend.

Nice.

Arobi Asaduzzaman
Zakariya Primary School, Forest Gate

All About Me

My name is Inam,
Sometimes I lead like an Imam.
The day I was born I accepted Islam,
My friends say that I am cool and calm.
My favourite sport is football,
I play it to become tall.
Even though I sometimes fall,
But do not bother at all.

I read my Sabaq regularly,
And then try to pray my Salah punctually,
And love to treat others kind-heartedly,
And make time for the Ummah particularly.
When I grow up I want to become coolness of my parents' eyes,
And shine like a glowing star in the sky.

Inamurrahman Mohammed
Zakariya Primary School, Forest Gate

I, Me And Myself

Roses are red,
Violets are blue,
I am sure you didn't get a due!

I am very caring,
But I dislike being primitive.

I never waste my precious time,
Because I find it a crime!

My favourite colour is orange,
My favourite mountain is Blomenge.

My favourite colour is green,
And for art, I am very keen.

This is me every day,
So please let me be this way!

Aaishah Rahamathaullah (10)
Zakariya Primary School, Forest Gate

The Cat In The Hat

Once we saw a house, and inside was one boy and
one girl.
A cat came and it was wearing a hat,
The colour was red and black.
The boy looked at him, the cat had a fish,
And a fly-ship.
They went with the cat,
They were in the zoo.
They saw a lion and a monkey,
One of the monkey's legs was hurt.
The cat, the boy and the girl were helping him,
The monkey felt better.

Muhammad Hassan (9)
Zakariya Primary School, Forest Gate

This Is Me Azaan

My name is Azaan,
And I have a little brother Amaan.
I like blue,
So as my baby brother too!
I like playing basketball,
Down in the hall.
I like to fly,
Way up in the sky.
My cheeks get red like the sun,
Because it's double the fun.
I am strong,
Like King Kong.
I am not fast,
I sometimes come last.

Azaan Al Islam Matubber
Zakariya Primary School, Forest Gate

Mohammed Biography

This is me, I like football.
I play for a team,
I like to run,
This is me.
I play video games,
This is me.
I like to help the teachers,
This is me.
My favourite food is pizza,
This is me.
I am the fastest in the class.
I like to box,
I am very strong,
I can knock out someone in one punch.

Mohammed Ismail (9)
Zakariya Primary School, Forest Gate

Happy Humaira

H umaira is my name,
U tterly smart and kind,
M y friends are Aishah and Manal,
A rt and maths are my favourites,
I am an expert on maths,
R eddish is the meaning of my name,
A nd I love my friends dearly.

Humaira Begum Ahmed (10)
Zakariya Primary School, Forest Gate

About Me

A m a student,
B ut I am trying for some improvement.
O wn me a school,
U phill for you.
T each me rhymes.

M y wish is mine,
E verybody and me want from God a sign.

Samir Mohammed (10)
Zakariya Primary School, Forest Gate

All About Me

Whenever I am down,
I play piano and learn something new.
I like to make raps,
And I like to read Harry Potter books.
I would love to be a doctor in the future.

Fatima Zahra (9)
Zakariya Primary School, Forest Gate

Manal Is My Name

M anal is my name,
A nger is not my game.
N ever hate yourself or others,
A nd never ever blame.
L ove your sisters and brothers.

Manal Said (10)
Zakariya Primary School, Forest Gate